BARRON'S

OGT

OHIO GRADUATION TEST IN READING AND WRITING

Steve Kucinski, M.S.
Masters in Educational Administration
Dublin Coffman High School
Newark, OH

BARRON'S

WITHDRAWN
FROM THE RODMAN PUBLIC LIBRARY

Copyright © 2008 by Barron's Educational Series, Inc.

All inquiries should be addressed to:
Barron's Educational Series, Inc.
250 Wireless Boulevard
Hauppauge, New York 11788
www.barronseduc.com

ISBN-13: 978-0-7641-3661-0
ISBN-10: 0-7641-3661-5

Library of Congress Catalog Card No. 2007030707

Library of Congress Cataloging-in-Publication Data

Kucinski, Steve.
  OGT in reading and writing / Steve Kucinski.
    p. cm.
  Includes index.
  ISBN-13: 978-0-7641-3661-0 (alk. paper)
  ISBN-10: 0-7641-3661-5 (alk. paper)
 1. Ohio Graduation Test—Study guides. 2. Examinations—Ohio—Study guides. 3. Reading—Examinations, questions, etc.   I. Title.

  LC1034.5.045K83 2008
  428.0071'2—dc22

                                                    2007030707

PRINTED IN THE UNITED STATES OF AMERICA

9 8 7 6 5 4 3 2 1

Introduction

If you're reading this, then you are preparing to take the Ohio Graduation Tests in all five areas: Reading, Math, Writing, Science, and Social Studies. This book is specifically designed to help you understand all the ins and outs of the Reading and Writing sections of the OGT. Students, parents, and teachers will find this a tremendously valuable resource. It is useful for learning what's on each test, how each section is scored, and how students can reach their maximum potential, especially if the "best" is not simply passing but achieving the accelerated or advanced range.

Students are often overheard saying, "Why do we have to take this?" The simple answer to that is "the State of Ohio says so!" But there's a bit more to it than that. The Proficiency Tests were replaced by the Ohio Graduation Tests and signed into law by Governor Taft in 2001. That same year, the State Board of Education adopted new academic content standards for English/Language Arts, and in 2002, the test was already being developed. And then, in March of 2005, the test was administered for the first time "for real."

So is the OGT a good thing? That depends on whom you're talking to. Students may not enjoy the pressure or the preparation, but parents and the community expect some accountability from the schools. The Ohio Graduation Tests are tools used to measure students' abilities and levels of competency in the specific academic content standards—they are not an evaluation of students as people. So, with that in mind, you should see that your hard work, your parents' hard work, your teachers' hard work, and the use of this book as a resource will help you to not only survive the Reading and Writing graduation tests, but to do your best as well!

Some of the following concepts will be stressed in this book:

- The academic content standards in English/Language Arts are well conceived; in all likelihood, your teachers use these standards to plan their lessons, so you are already "doing the stuff" that you're being asked to do on the Reading and Writing graduation tests, anyway.

- Not all of the content standards are represented on the tests; this book will focus on helping students to know what skills the standards are testing. Some parts of the tests require previous knowledge and skills, and some simply are an "on the spot" performance. You will need to know which are which!

- Students can improve scores by using some common sense strategies, such as highlighting, note taking, and knowing how the test is scored. And, as a bonus, those are the same skills that will help you score well on the PSAT, ACT, and SAT!

- There are five ranges of performance levels on the tests: "limited" and "basic," which are considered failing; and "passing," "accelerated," and "advanced." This book focuses on helping students pass, but the information and exercises in here will allow you to reach the level that shows your true potential.

There's much in store for you as you begin your journey of preparation. As Confucius said, "A journey of a thousand miles begins with a single step." Some of this may seem easy to you; during those times, enjoy it because you've earned that right, but focus on getting every single question correct <u>and</u> knowing how and why it's correct. During the parts where you struggle, try to determine the issue. Is it the reading passage or the wording of the questions in the Reading section? Is it the wording of the prompt in the Writing test? Figuring out where and why you're stuck is just as important in helping you to do your best as is answering questions correctly. Remember that Confucius also said, "I hear and I forget. I see and I remember. I do and I understand." This book is certainly about "seeing" and a lot about "doing" and "understanding." After completing it, you'll feel proud of yourself and your work, and when you get your results, you will know that they truly reflect your maximum reading and writing potential!

Suit up and get ready to take the court. NBA legend Michael Jordan said, "I've always believed that if you put in the work, the results will come. I don't do things half-heartedly. Because I know if I do, then I can expect half-hearted results." Follow this guide, work hard, and the results *will* come. Mr. Jordan also said, "Just play. Have fun. Enjoy the game." Let the game begin, and enjoy!

Contents

The Basics

Before you begin using the book, let's check your background knowledge on some testing terms. Quiz yourself by covering the right half of the page to see if you can come up with a decent definition yourself.

Test-Related Word	Meaning
Analyze	To examine the different parts of a problem
Compare	To find out what is alike and what is different.
Describe	To give information about
Evaluate	To determine the value of something
Explain	To give a reason for something
Formulate	To review information and present an idea
Infer	To form an opinion beyond what is directly stated
Predict	To make a statement about something that has not happened
Summarize	To explain the major parts of
Support	To provide evidence that proves something
Trace	To show the path of something

HOT OFF THE PRESS—NOTES AND TIPS FROM THE MARCH 2007 READING AND WRITING OGT

One of the advantages that you will have with this practice resource is that the OGT has been administered to students for several years. Each year, the State of Ohio releases the previous year's test along with the answers and guides as to how the written portions should be scored. Whenever possible, those have been consulted to make this guide very closely aligned with the "real thing."

Each year there are changes in the types of questions presented on the test, and this first section is designed to highlight elements that are brand new and worth your immediate attention as of the most recent administration of the OGT—March, 2007.

NEW POINTS OF EMPHASIS FOR THE READING TEST

This past year's Reading test focused on some of the less common parts of each standard (full standards are presented at the beginning of each chapter). For example, there were questions about advertisements and their effectiveness. Also, there were questions about the trustworthiness and reputation of a business.

On this past year's Reading OGT, the students were frequently given additional information about the questions after the title, referred to as "headnotes." These are important because they are easy to skip over on one's way to the question, but often the test questions involved the information in the headnote. For example, a headnote could read, "This poster was created by Bob Smith for his store that sells donuts. He used bright colors and large print to catch your attention."

The question then is "What is the purpose of the headnote?" It's really a simple question, but first you would need to know what the term "headnote" means, and then you'd have to have read the headnote and decided that it simply provides background information on the creator and the poster. Not too tough, but easy to overlook.

For passages that have headnotes but no direct questions about them, read them carefully anyway. They have background information about the author, time period, or reading selection that can help you answer some of the questions.

Something else worth noting about the latest Reading OGT is that many of the questions are of the type that ask the reader to use his or her judgment rather than look back in the passage for the detail. This means that you'll see words in the question like "infer," "suggest," "imply," and "probably." You will practice all of these in this resource, but be prepared to see more of these types in the test. Certain students prefer questions that have answers that they can "put their finger on" in the text, but you should feel confident that you will have all the tools you need to answer any of the more challenging questions, too.

SYNTHESIS QUESTION

This sounds scary, but it simply means that you are being asked to take your knowledge of one passage and combine it with your knowledge of another passage. In the 2007 Reading OGT, students were asked to compare two characters, one from a prose passage and another from a poem.

This was a 2-point short-answer question; we will discuss how to get all of the points on every written question later. For now, keep in mind that you would get one point for providing a plausible or reasonable answer, and another point for referring to specific information from both texts. This will seem to take you enough time that you feel it's worth more than 2 points, but remember that it's worth it to get full points on every single written question.

NEW POINTS OF EMPHASIS FOR THE WRITING TEST

On the March 2007 Writing OGT, there were more questions than ever before about the organization of writing. For example, students were asked about appropriate topic sentences to use for certain paragraphs. Also, they were given a sample paragraph and asked what type of organization was used. Choices for such a question can involve compare/contrast, chronological (time), classification (type), and spatial (dealing with location or relationships). Like much of the test, it's easier than it might seem to answer questions like this correctly. It's all part of taking your time to think and following what you already know, all of which this book will show you how to do successfully.

The chart below represents the score ranges from the March 2007 OGT.

Subject	Performance Level	Raw Score	Scaled Score
Reading	Advanced	39.5–48.0	448–549
	Accelerated	33.0–39.0	429–447
	Proficient	20.0–32.5	400–428
	Basic	13.0–19.5	383–399
	Limited	0.0–12.5	260–382
Writing	Advanced	43.0–48.0	476–560
	Accelerated	34.0–42.5	430–475
	Proficient	25.0–33.5	400–429
	Basic	17.0–24.5	378–399
	Limited	0.0–16.5	276–377

The chart below represents the scores and achievement levels for all Ohio students who took the March 2007 Reading and Writing graduation tests. As you can see, 86.7% "passed" the Reading OGT (a decrease from 89.2 in 2006), and 89.3% "passed" the Writing OGT (an increase from 88.0 in 2006). However, this chart does not indicate if they barely passed, or reached the Advanced or Accelerated categories. That will be our goal with this resource—to help you to reach your maximum potential.

Reading

Performance Level		Number	Percent
Proficient or above:	Advanced	16,058	11.7	86.7
	Accelerated	42,238	30.8	
	Proficient	60,488	44.2	
Below proficient:	Basic	11,645	8.5	13.3
	Limited	6,529	4.8	

Writing

Performance Level		Number	Percent	
Proficient or above:	Advanced	1,945	1.4	89.3
	Accelerated	71,298	52.3	
	Proficient	48,499	35.6	
Below proficient:	Basic	10,972	8.0	10.7
	Limited	3,685	2.7	

The following tables describe the different ranges you can score on each of the five graduation tests. With this resource, you will be able to maximize your potential and score in the Advanced or Accelerated range for both the Reading and Writing tests. Read through the descriptions paying close attention to the words in bold print. That is what makes the skill sets different for the categories. Where do you think you stand on each one right now?

Performance Level Descriptors—Reading

Accelerated	Students performing at the Accelerated level use their understanding of word structure, context clues, and text structures to determine the meaning of unfamiliar or complex words. They show an **overall understanding** and make **evaluative and analytical judgments** of textual information. Students are able to **explain and analyze** the various ways authors may influence text and **assess the appropriateness** of provided information.
Proficient	Students performing at the Proficient level use their basic understanding of word structure, context clues, and text structures to determine the meaning of unfamiliar or complex words. They can **typically** show an overall understanding of and make **evaluative** judgments of textual information. Students are **generally able** to identify and explain the various ways authors may influence text and assess the appropriateness of provided information.
Basic	Students performing at the Basic level can **generally** define unfamiliar or complex words through contextual clues and can determine resources to define or understand the more complex words. They can demonstrate **some understanding**, and are able **to make some interpretations and judgments** of textual information.
Limited	Students performing at the Limited level demonstrate skill and understanding **below the performance required to reach the Basic level**.

Performance Level Descriptors—Writing

Advanced	Students performing at the Advanced level demonstrate a **superior** understanding of the *writing process* and a **superior** grasp of the purpose of *writing and writing style*. They demonstrate **exceptional skills** at *organizing, revising, and editing* writing. The students write with an **exceptional** *focus and engage* a reader through exceptionally *well-developed, unified, and coherent ideas*. The students use *sentence variety* and make effective *word choices* with a high degree of **consistency**. They also understand *grammar, capitalization, punctuation, and spelling conventions* at the same high degree of **consistency.**
Accelerated	Students performing at the Accelerated level demonstrate an **excellent** understanding of the writing process and an **excellent** grasp of the purpose of writing and writing style. They demonstrate **well-developed** skills at organizing, revising, and editing writing. The students write with a well-developed focus and engage a reader through well-developed, unified, and coherent ideas. The students use sentence variety and make effective word choices with consistency. They also consistently understand grammar, capitalization, punctuation, and spelling conventions.
Proficient	Students performing at the Proficient level demonstrate an **adequate to effective** understanding of the writing process and an **adequate to effective** grasp of the purpose of writing and writing style. They demonstrate **developed** skills at organizing, revising, and editing writing. The students write with a **reasonably well-developed** focus and engage a reader through **reasonably well-developed**, unified, and coherent ideas. The students use sentence variety and make **effective** word choices with **some consistency**. They also, with **some consistency**, understand grammar, capitalization, punctuation, and spelling conventions.
Basic	Students performing at the Basic level demonstrate a **marginal** understanding of the writing process and a **marginal** grasp of the purpose of writing and style. They demonstrate **some skills** at organizing, revising, and editing writing. The students write with **some focus** and engage a reader through **a few** developed, unified, and coherent ideas. The students use **some** sentence variety and make effective word choices inconsistently. They also have a **marginal** understanding of grammar, capitalization, punctuation, and spelling conventions.
Limited	Students performing at the Limited level demonstrate skills and understanding **below the performance required to reach the Basic level.**

Diagnostic Test: OGT in Reading

Before you begin practicing and honing your skills, read the following passage and complete the diagnostic questions. After completing the questions, review the answers and the corresponding skills and benchmarks. This is not a full-blown practice OGT; it is designed to diagnose specific areas of reading and comprehension. This will help you fine-tune where your strengths and weaknesses are so that you can keep them in mind as you complete the book and the practice tests at the end.

Directions: As you read, mark any words that are unfamiliar to you, and keep notes in the margins about questions you have or reactions you have to the story.

Parts of the story will be marked with numbers that will correspond to the diagnostic questions. This will help you to look up answers and track where and how to locate information.

"The Lady or the Tiger"
Frank Stockton 1882

1   In the very olden time there lived a semi-barbaric king, whose ideas, though somewhat polished and sharpened by the progressiveness of distant Latin neighbors, were still large, florid, and untrammeled, as became the half of him which was barbaric. He was a man of exuberant fancy, and, withal, of an authority so irresistible that, at his will, he turned his varied fancies into facts. He was greatly given to self-communing, and, when he and himself agreed upon anything, the thing was done. When every member of his domestic and political systems moved smoothly in its appointed course, his nature was bland and genial; but, whenever there was a little hitch, and some of his orbs got out of their orbits, he was blander and more genial still, for nothing pleased him so much as to make the crooked straight and crush down uneven places.

2 Among the borrowed notions by which his barbarism had become semified was that of the public arena, in which, by exhibitions of manly and beastly valor, the minds of his subjects were refined and cultured. But even here the exuberant and barbaric fancy asserted itself. The arena of the king was built, not to give the people an opportunity of hearing the rhapsodies of dying gladiators, nor to enable them to view the inevitable conclusion of a conflict between religious opinions and hungry jaws, but for purposes far better adapted to widen and develop the mental energies of the people. This vast amphitheater, with its encircling galleries, its mysterious vaults, and its unseen passages, was an agent of poetic justice, in which crime was punished, or virtue rewarded, by the decrees of an impartial and incorruptible chance.

3 When a subject was accused of a crime of sufficient importance to interest the king, public notice was given that on an appointed day the fate of the accused person would be decided in the king's arena, a structure which well deserved its name, for, although its form and plan were borrowed from afar, its purpose emanated solely from the brain of this man, who, every barley-corn a king, knew no tradition to which he owed more allegiance than pleased his fancy, and who ingrafted on every adopted form of human thought and action the rich growth of his barbaric idealism. When all the people had assembled in the galleries, and the king, surrounded by his court, sat high up on his throne of royal state on one side of the arena, he gave a signal, a door beneath him opened, and the accused subject stepped out into the amphitheater. Directly opposite him, on the other side of the enclosed space, were two doors, exactly alike and side by side. It was the duty and the privilege of the person on trial to walk directly to these doors and open one of them. He could open either door he pleased; he was subject to no guidance or influence but that of the aforementioned impartial and incorruptible chance. If he opened the one, there came out of it a hungry tiger, the fiercest and most cruel that could be procured, which immediately sprang upon him and tore him to pieces as a punishment for his guilt. The moment that the case of the criminal was thus decided, doleful iron bells were clanged, great wails went up from the hired mourners posted on the outer rim of the arena, and the vast audience, with bowed heads and downcast hearts, wended slowly their homeward way, mourning greatly that one so young and fair, or so old and respected, should have merited so dire a fate.

4 But, if the accused person opened the other door, there came forth from it a lady, the most suitable to his years and station that his majesty could select among his fair subjects, and to this lady he was immediately married, as a reward of his innocence. It mattered not that he might already possess a wife and family, or that his affections might be engaged upon an object of his own selection; the king allowed no such subordinate arrangements to interfere with his great scheme of *retribution* and reward. The exercises, as in the other instance, took place immediately, and in the arena. Another door opened beneath the king, and a priest, followed by a band of choristers, and dancing maidens blowing joyous airs on golden horns and treading an epithalamic measure, advanced to where the pair stood, side by side, and the wedding was promptly and cheerily solemnized. Then the gay brass bells

rang forth their merry peals, the people shouted glad hurrahs, and the inno-cent man, preceded by children strewing flowers on his path, led his bride to his home.

5   This was the king's semi-barbaric method of administering justice. Its per-fect fairness is obvious. The criminal could not know out of which door would come the lady; he opened either he pleased, without having the slightest idea whether, in the next instant, he was to be devoured or mar-ried. On some occasions the tiger came out of one door, and on some out of the other. The decisions of this tribunal were not only fair, they were pos-itively determinate: the accused person was instantly punished if he found himself guilty, and, if innocent, he was rewarded on the spot, whether he liked it or not. There was no escape from the judgments of the king's arena.

6   The institution was a very popular one. When the people gathered together on one of the great trial days, they never knew whether they were to witness a bloody slaughter or a hilarious wedding. This element of uncertainty lent an interest to the occasion which it could not otherwise have attained. Thus, the masses were entertained and pleased, and the thinking part of the com-munity could bring no charge of unfairness against this plan, for did not the accused person have the whole matter in his own hands? This semi-barbaric king had a daughter as blooming as his most florid fancies, and with a soul as fervent and imperious as his own. As is usual in such cases, she was the apple of his eye, and was loved by him above all humanity. Among his courtiers was a young man of that fineness of blood and lowness of station common to the conventional heroes of romance who love royal maidens. This royal maiden was well satisfied with her lover, for he was handsome and brave to a degree unsurpassed in all this kingdom, and she loved him with an ardor that had enough of barbarism in it to make it exceedingly warm and strong. This love affair moved on happily for many months, until one day the king happened to discover its existence. He did not hesitate nor waver in regard to his duty in the premises. The youth was immediately cast into prison, and a day was appointed for his trial in the king's arena. This, of course, was an especially important occasion, and his majesty, as well as all the people, was greatly interested in the workings and development of this trial. Never before had such a case occurred; never before had a subject dared to love the daughter of the king. In after years such things became commonplace enough, but then they were in no slight degree novel and startling.

7   The tiger-cages of the kingdom were searched for the most savage and relentless beasts, from which the fiercest monster might be selected for the arena; and the ranks of maiden youth and beauty throughout the land were carefully surveyed by competent judges in order that the young man might have a fitting bride in case fate did not determine for him a different des-tiny. Of course, everybody knew that the deed with which the accused was charged had been done. He had loved the princess, and neither he, she, nor any one else, thought of denying the fact; but the king would not think of allowing any fact of this kind to interfere with the workings of the tribunal, in which he took such great delight and satisfaction. No matter how the affair turned out, the youth would be disposed of, and the king would take an aesthetic pleasure in watching the course of events, which would deter-

mine whether or not the young man had done wrong in allowing himself to love the princess.

8   The appointed day arrived. From far and near the people gathered, and thronged the great galleries of the arena, and crowds, unable to gain admittance, massed themselves against its outside walls. The king and his court were in their places, opposite the twin doors, those fateful portals, so terrible in their similarity. All was ready. The signal was given. A door beneath the royal party opened, and the lover of the princess walked into the arena. Tall, beautiful, fair, his appearance was greeted with a low hum of admiration and anxiety. Half the audience had not known so grand a youth had lived among them. No wonder the princess loved him! What a terrible thing for him to be there!

9   As the youth advanced into the arena he turned, as the custom was, to bow to the king, but he did not think at all of that royal personage. His eyes were fixed upon the princess, who sat to the right of her father. Had it not been for the moiety* of barbarism in her nature it is probable that lady would not have been there, but her intense and fervid soul would not allow her to be absent on an occasion in which she was so terribly interested. From the moment that the decree had gone forth that her lover should decide his fate in the king's arena, she had thought of nothing, night or day, but this great event and the various subjects connected with it. Possessed of more power, influence, and force of character than any one who had ever before been interested in such a case, she had done what no other person had done— she had possessed herself of the secret of the doors. She knew in which of the two rooms, that lay behind those doors, stood the cage of the tiger, with its open front, and in which waited the lady. Through these thick doors, heavily curtained with skins on the inside, it was impossible that any noise or suggestion should come from within to the person who should approach to raise the latch of one of them. But gold, and the power of a woman's will, had brought the secret to the princess.

10   And not only did she know in which room stood the lady ready to emerge, all blushing and radiant, should her door be opened, but she knew who the lady was. It was one of the fairest and loveliest of the damsels of the court who had been selected as the reward of the accused youth, should he be proved innocent of the crime of aspiring to one so far above him; and the princess hated her. Often had she seen, or imagined that she had seen, this fair creature throwing glances of admiration upon the person of her lover, and sometimes she thought these glances were perceived, and even returned. Now and then she had seen them talking together; it was but for a moment or two, but much can be said in a brief space; it may have been on most unimportant topics, but how could she know that? The girl was lovely, but she had dared to raise her eyes to the loved one of the princess; and, with all the intensity of the savage blood transmitted to her through long lines of wholly barbaric ancestors, she hated the woman who blushed and trembled behind that silent door.

---

*part

11 When her lover turned and looked at her, and his eye met hers as she sat there, paler and whiter than any one in the vast ocean of anxious faces about her, he saw, by that power of quick perception which is given to those whose souls are one, that she knew behind which door crouched the tiger, and behind which stood the lady. He had expected her to know it. He understood her nature, and his soul was assured that she would never rest until she had made plain to herself this thing, hidden to all other lookers-on, even to the king. The only hope for the youth in which there was any element of certainty was based upon the success of the princess in discovering this mystery; and the moment he looked upon her, he saw she had succeeded, as in his soul he knew she would succeed.

Then it was that his quick and anxious glance asked the question: "Which?" It was as plain to her as if he shouted it from where he stood. There was not an instant to be lost. The question was asked in a flash; it must be answered in another.

Her right arm lay on the cushioned parapet before her. She raised her hand, and made a slight, quick movement toward the right. No one but her lover saw her. Every eye but his was fixed on the man in the arena.

He turned, and with a firm and rapid step he walked across the empty space. Every heart stopped beating, every breath was held, every eye was fixed immovably upon that man. Without the slightest hesitation, he went to the door on the right, and opened it.

12 Now, the point of the story is this: Did the tiger come out of that door, or did the lady ? The more we reflect upon this question, the harder it is to answer. It involves a study of the human heart which leads us through devious mazes of passion, out of which it is difficult to find our way. Think of it, fair reader, not as if the decision of the question depended upon yourself, but upon that hot-blooded, semi-barbaric princess, her soul at a white heat beneath the combined fires of despair and jealousy. She had lost him, but who should have him? How often, in her waking hours and in her dreams, had she started in wild horror, and covered her face with her hands as she thought of her lover opening the door on the other side of which waited the cruel fangs of the tiger!

13 But how much oftener had she seen him at the other door! How in her grievous reveries had she gnashed her teeth, and torn her hair, when she saw his start of rapturous delight as he opened the door of the lady! How her soul had burned in agony when she had seen him rush to meet that woman, with her flushing cheek and sparkling eye of triumph; when she had seen him lead her forth, his whole frame kindled with the joy of recovered life; when she had heard the glad shouts from the multitude, and the wild ringing of the happy bells; when she had seen the priest, with his joyous followers, advance to the couple, and make them man and wife before her very eyes; and when she had seen them walk away together upon their path of flowers, followed by the tremendous shouts of the hilarious multitude, in which her one despairing shriek was lost and drowned! Would it not be better for him to die at once, and go to wait for her in the blessed regions of semi-barbaric futurity?

And yet, that awful tiger, those shrieks, that blood!

Her decision had been indicated in an instant, but it had been made after days and nights of anguished deliberation. She had known she would be asked, she had decided what she would answer, and, without the slightest hesitation, she had moved her hand to the right.

14 The question of her decision is one not to be lightly considered, and it is not for me to presume to set myself up as the one person able to answer it. And so I leave it with all of you: Which came out of the opened door—the lady, or the tiger?

1. Explain what the term *retribution* means as it is used in the following passage from the text: "It mattered not that he might already possess a wife and family, or that his affections might be engaged upon an object of his own selection; the king allowed no such subordinate arrangements to interfere with his great scheme of *retribution* and reward." Provide an example or context clue from the passage to support your response.

_____

_____

_____

_____

_____

2. In paragraph 1, what attitude characterizes the king's approach to ruling his kingdom?

   A. weak
   B. stubborn
   C. democratic
   D. progressive

3. Why is the princess unsure about telling her lover which door to choose?

   A. She is not sure if she wants him to marry a woman she hates.
   B. She does not really like the young man.
   C. She can't stand the sight of blood.
   D. She can't quite remember which door is which.

4. The princess signals her lover about the door by

   A. winking her right eye.
   B. lifting her right foot.
   C. wearing an earring only in the right ear.
   D. raising her right hand and gesturing to the right.

5. What is ironic about the princess' reaction to the event in the arena?

   A. She secretly wanted to be in this position all along.
   B. She hesitates when it is in her power to save her lover's life.
   C. She is typically outspoken but remains quiet when it is important.
   D. She always does everything her father asks her to do.

6. The author leaves the ending of the story open in order to

   A. frustrate the reader.
   B. allow the reader to think about human nature.
   C. add humor and sarcasm to the story.
   D. keep from having to decide the ending himself.

7. When the author says (in paragraph 6) "Thus, the masses were entertained and pleased, and the thinking part of the community could bring no charge of unfairness against this plan, for did not the accused person have the whole matter in his own hands?" what is implied about the fairness of the process?

   A. It is unfair because the person can be eaten by a tiger.
   B. It is fair because there is only one dangerous outcome.
   C. It is fair because the person accused gets to choose for himself.
   D. it is unfair because there is no discussion involved.

8. Read the following excerpt from paragraph 7 of the passage.

   "Of course, everybody knew that the deed with which the accused was charged had been done. He had loved the princess, and neither he, she, nor any one else, thought of denying the fact; but the king would not think of allowing any fact of this kind to interfere with the workings of the tribunal, in which he took such great delight and satisfaction."

   This excerpt can best be summarized by which sentence?

   A. The accused was hated by the members of the kingdom for loving the princess.
   B. The king felt sorry for the accused because he loved his daughter so much.
   C. The accused had tried to deny loving the princess.
   D. Even though the accused loved his daughter, the king makes him go through the process in the arena.

9. The author uses the simile and metaphor combination "...and his eye met hers as she sat there paler and whiter *than* any one of the vast *ocean of anxious faces* about her . . ." (paragraph 10) in order to

    A. show that the princess was scared.

    B. prove that the members of the kingdom were truly barbaric.

    C. show how many people were there.

    D. show that there was water around the kingdom.

10. Which sentence gives an important idea in the passage?

    A. Kings can be barbaric at times.

    B. Jealousy can make a person do strange things.

    C. Using chance to determine justice is fair.

    D. Two people who love each other should be left alone.

11. According to the passage, which conclusion can be inferred about the narrator's attitude towards the young accused lover?

    A. He is a good man and should not be punished simply for loving the princess.

    B. He made a mistake and should accept his punishment.

    C. He does not truly love the princess.

    D. He should run away to avoid possibly being killed by the tiger.

12. Which explanation suggests the author's purpose in describing the difficulty the princess has in making up her mind about helping the accused?

    A. to portray the princess as cold and unfeeling.

    B. to let the reader see the princess as having realistic emotions.

    C. to add suspense to the story.

    D. to teach the reader the correct way to make decisions.

13. For the author, the two doors represent

    A. the two different paths one can take in life.

    B. the difference between death and life with another person.

    C. the choice between selfishness and selflessness.

    D. the ability to make a choice to determine someone else's fate.

14. This story is told from whose point of view?

    A. the king's

    B. the princess'

    C. the narrator's

    D. the accused's

15. What is implied by the following phrase (from paragraph 9) "But gold, and the power of a woman's will, had brought the secret to the princess"?

    A. The princess accidentally found out what was behind each door.

    B. The princess had bribed and convinced someone to tell her what was behind each door.

    C. The princess would have traded gold to save the accused.

    D. The princess is very pushy and very wealthy.

Answers, explanations, and diagnostic tools for the OGT in Reading

Acquisition of Vocabulary/part 3—discussed in Chapter 2

1. This question was phrased in the style of a 2-point short-answer question, which we will discuss in Chapter 6. The vocabulary of this short story is fairly sophisticated, which is good because that is the way the OGT has leaned the last couple of years. For this question, you need to have written down what you think the word "retribution" means in the given example. Since it is about how the king administered justice, using chance and two different doors (one positive and one negative), you are looking for opposites. The word means "punishment," and a context clue for that is that it is followed by its opposite, "reward," in the excerpt. There are other types of vocabulary questions on the Reading OGT, and we will practice all of them in Chapter 2.

Reading Applications: Literary Text/part 3—discussed in Chapter 5

2. **(B)** While the word "stubborn" is not used directly, if you re-read paragraph 1, you will see it notes about the king, ". . . when he and himself agreed upon anything, it was done." It is certainly not A, "weak." Kings are not likely to be C, "democratic." The word "progressive" is mentioned, but it is in regards to comparing the king to his "distant Latin neighbors." This type of question can be challenging, since you are being asked to make an inference. Much more practice on this skill is available in Chapter 5.

Reading Applications: Literary Text/part 1—discussed in Chapter 5

3. **(A)** B, C, and D are not supported in the text, and the princess' negative feelings about the woman behind the door are explained in paragraph 9. Questions like this one aren't too tough if you take your time and think about what you've read. Chapter 5 will also help you to practice questions like this one.

Reading Process/part 3—discussed in Chapter 3

4. **(D)** This is a detail question, and it is directly stated in the text (paragraph 10). Because of this, you should always be able to get these correct if you are willing to take your time. Some additional practice will be coming in Chapter 3.

Reading Applications: Literary Text/part 9—discussed in Chapter 5

5. **(B)** In order to find the correct answer, you have to know the different types of irony (discussed in Chapter 5). In this case, it is situational irony, because the narrator spends so much time talking about the strong love between the princess and the accused, yet she hesitates when she has the chance to save his life. The correct answer, therefore, is B.

Reading Applications: Literary Text/part 13—discussed in Chapter 5

6. **(B)** This type of question is challenging because it asks you to think as if you were the author. A and D seem a little far-fetched. While C is possible, because

it can be considered humorous that the ending is not explained, given the way the author phrases it, B is a better answer.

Technical and Persuasive Text/part 5—discussed in Chapter 4

7. **(C)** This question is complicated because of its several steps. You have to read the excerpt given and then think about what is implied (not directly stated). Because the excerpt discusses the fact that no matter what happens, it was through the choice of the accused person, C is the correct answer. Author's intent and what he or she implies is discussed more in Chapter 4, especially in terms of non-fiction writing.

Reading Process/part 1—discussed in Chapter 3

8. **(D)** This one was not as tough as it may have looked. You had to read the given excerpt but then were simply asked to summarize it. Summaries should be broad enough to include the main idea of the excerpt. They must also be accurate. The correct answer here is D.

Acquisition of Vocabulary/part 1—discussed in Chapter 2

9. **(A)** This question requires you to understand some basic figurative language, simile and metaphor in this case. A is the best answer because it covers both the simile and metaphor (white face and many people = princess is scared). C is close, but it only covers the metaphor of an "ocean of faces." You will be asked questions about figurative language in poetry, which will be discussed in Chapter 5, but examples can also be pulled out of the context of the written passages, which is part of Chapter 2.

Reading Process/part 1—discussed in Chapter 3

10. **(B)** If you think about it, much has already been said about this concept in other questions. We know that the princess hesitated about saving the accused from a previous question. Also, A, C, and D are either not necessarily noted in the passage or do not qualify as "important" ideas. Think of this as a question about the "theme" of the story, which you are typically asked to discuss in any English class. Chapter 3 will discuss this in more detail.

Technical and Persuasive Text/part 5—discussed in Chapter 4

11. **(A)** This is another complicated question. It involves the narrator's attitude and making an inference. The answer, though, is pretty obvious in this case. At the end of paragraph 7, the narrator states about the accused entering the arena, "What a terrible thing for him to have to be there!" This makes choice A clearly the best answer. This type of question is easy to miss, so pay close attention to the discussion in Chapter 4, especially as it pertains to non-fiction.

Technical and Persuasive Text/part 6—discussed in Chapter 4

12. **(B)** This "author's purpose" question can be tricky, especially if you feel awkward making assumptions about what is on the mind of an author. Again, some

aspects of this part of the story have been addressed in other questions so far—use that to your advantage. B is the best answer, especially if you think back to question 10 about jealousy and its being an important idea in the story.

Reading Applications: Literary Text/part 11—discussed in Chapter 5

13. **(C)** This question is about symbolism or something representing another item or concept. Much of the story focuses on the princess and what she experiences because she knows what is behind each door. She also has the power to tell the accused and so control his fate. Because she does not seem to want to accept that her lover might be saved but marry a woman the princess hates, allowing him to live would be a selfless act. Allowing him to die so she doesn't have to feel awkward would be a selfish act. Choice C is the most accurate answer here. These can be tough, because symbols can mean different things to different people. Chapter 5 will assist you in being successful with this type of question.

Reading Applications: Literary Text/part 5—discussed in Chapter 5

14. **(C)** This question is about point of view and is pretty straightforward. Since we know what is happening everywhere and what each character is thinking and feeling, it is considered "omniscient," and this can only be accomplished through the C, "narrator's" point of view.

Reading Applications: Literary Text/part 13—discussed in Chapter 5

15. **(B)** Here again you have a question with multiple steps. You have to read the excerpt and think about what it is implying. This means, you will not be able to put your finger on the answer in the text—you are going to have to assume, using your judgment and what you've read and understood in the story. The excerpt does not state it directly, but it mentions that the princess finds out about the doors using "gold" and the "power of a woman's will." This can be broken down into money and being persuasive and persistent. The answer that best corresponds to this is B. This is a good example of a question where the answer is actually right there if you think about it, even though it does not appear to state it directly like a detail question.

You may have noticed that many of the questions come from Reading Applications: Literary Text in Chapter 5. The Reading OGT is indeed heavy in this category because it involves many different skills. Two good pieces of news are that you do much of this every year in your English class and other classes. And you will get much support and practice in this book in Chapter 5 and on the practice tests. If you missed many of these questions, take your time and linger on every page in this chapter.

Check out the rest of your results on the diagnostic. Do you see any trends? You can keep track of which questions you missed and remember to keep this in mind as you progress through the book, so that you can spend extra time and energy on those chapters. This will make the practice tests at the end more meaningful and useful. Let's see how your skills rate in the areas of writing.

Diagnostic Test: OGT in Writing

Complete the diagnostic questions for the OGT in Writing. After completing the questions, review the answers and the corresponding skills and benchmarks. This is not a full-blown practice OGT; it is designed to diagnose specific areas in which you need to concentrate your efforts. This will help you fine-tune where your strengths and weaknesses are so that you can keep them in mind as you complete the book and the practice tests at the end.

Directions: Follow the same procedure for this test as you did with the Reading diagnostic. Remember, this is not a practice test but you should take each question seriously so that you can get some gauge as to your strengths and areas of improvement in Writing.

1. Which would be an appropriate topic sentence for a paragraph about categories of sports?
   A. There are many different types of sports.
   B. People can play sports in parks.
   C. Sports are classified by where and how they are played.
   D. Baseball is a fun sport.

2. Read the paragraph and decide what type of organization is being used.

   When I woke up that morning, I knew it was going to be a great day. First, I had my favorite breakfast, and I was able to catch a few minutes of cartoons on television. When I got to school, I got an essay back with an A on it. After school, I was allowed to play with my friends until dinner time, and I even got to stay up a little later to hang out with my sister who was home from college. Yes, it certainly was a great day.

   A. chronological
   B. comparison/contrast
   C. spatial
   D. classification

3. Which sentence appropriately utilizes precise language and eliminates wordiness to convey what Jill should do?

    A. Jill should sing and dance.
    B. Jill should sing and dance, if time permits.
    C. Jill needs sing, and then if she has the time, she should dance.
    D. Jill should sing, and then if she has any time left over, she should dance.

Read the draft paragraph and answer questions 4 and 5.

(1) My friend Bill and I got us a new board game to play. (2) My mother gave me the game thinking it would be fun. (3) We hadn't hardly begun playing when Bill discovered that he did not have the complete directions. (4) We had already walked to his house, which was a mile away from mine. (5) After we walked back to my house, we were tired and grouchy.

4. In the context of the paragraph, which is the correct way to revise and/or edit sentence 1?

    A. My friend Bill and I got a new board game to play.
    B. I and my friend Bill got a new board game to play.
    C. My friend Bill and me got a new board game to play.
    D. My friend Bill and me got us a new board game to play.

5. In the context of the paragraph, which is the correct way to revise and/or edit sentence 3?

    A. We had hardly begun playing Bill discovered that he did not have the complete directions.
    B. We had hardly begun playing when Bill discovered that he did not have the complete directions.
    C. We had not hardly begun playing when Bill discovered that he did not have the complete directions.
    D. Bill discovered that he did not have the complete directions when we had hardly begun playing.

6. Which would be the appropriate revision and/or edit to the sentence below for an elementary school audience?

    It has recently been discovered that exposing vegetable plants to varying types of colored lights may affect the size of vegetables they produce.

    A. If you want plants to produce the largest vegetables, you should put them under colored lights.
    B. Plants grown under green lights produce larger vegetables than plants grown under red lights.
    C. Research has shown that vegetable production varies in relation to the color of light under which they are grown.
    D. It has been shown that plants produce larger vegetables when grown under green lights than they do when grown under red lights.

Read the draft paragraph and answer questions 7 and 8.

(1) Last night my city had the best fireworks display I had ever seen. (2) Looking up the fireworks were bright and filled the entire sky. (3) All of my friends's houses were lit up with each boom. (4) The whole town looked like a rock concert!

7. In the context of the paragraph, what is the correct way to revise sentence 2?

    A. When I looked up, the fireworks were bright and filled the entire sky.
    B. Filling up the sky were the fireworks as I looked up.
    C. When I looked up, fireworks filled the entire sky, and they were bright.
    D. Looking up, I saw the fireworks, and they filled the sky and were bright.

8. In the context of the paragraph, what is the correct way to revise sentence 3?

    A. All of my friend's houses were lit up with each boom.
    B. All of my friend's houses was lit up with each boom.
    C. All of my friends' houses were lit up with each boom.
    D. All of my friends houses were lit up with each boom.

Use the following information from a handbook on language to answer question 9.

Use a comma

- to separate three or more words, phrases or clauses in a series: She brought a tent, a sleeping bag, and firewood.
- to separate adjectives that equally modify the same noun: She was a young, happy girl.
- to set off introductory words, phrases or clauses from the rest of the sentence: Sadly, it rained during her camping trip.
- to set off parenthetical elements: She was, you might expect, happy to pack up and go home.

9. Which is the correct way to edit the sentence below?

    The long rainy camping trip caused the girl to want to stay very close to home the following week.

    A. The long rainy camping trip caused the girl to want to stay very, close to home the following week.
    B. The long, rainy, camping trip caused the girl to want to stay very close to home the following week.
    C. The long, rainy camping trip caused the girl to want to stay very close to home the following week.
    D. The long rainy, camping trip caused the girl to want to stay very close to home the following week.

10. John is writing a paper tracing the movement of glaciers in North America.

    Which resource or reference would enhance the quality of his paper?

    A. dictionary
    B. personal interviews
    C. atlas
    D. thesaurus

Answers, explanations, and diagnostic tools for the OGT in Writing

Writing Processes/ part 8

1. **(C)** For this question, you need a sentence that is about categories of sports, but it should not be too broad or too specific. A is too broad. B is off-topic. D is too narrow because it's only about one sport. C is the best answer because it is open to all sports and mentions how they are classified. It is a solid topic sentence. This is one of many standards in the Writing Processes category, all of which will be discussed and practiced both in Chapter 8 and in the two practice tests at the end.

Writing Processes/ part 6

2. **(A)** The toughest part of this question is the answer choices. If you break each one down, though, this one becomes quite obvious. "Chronological" means based on time. "Comparison/contrast" speaks for itself. "Spatial" has to do with spacing or how things are physically arranged. "Classification" involves grouping something together with others. Because the sample paragraph is about a person's daily life, A, "chronological," is the best answer.

Writing Processes/ part 9

3. **(B)** This type of question can be more difficult than one with errors in grammar or spelling. Remember that you are looking for clear and understandable wording. B is the best answer in this case. A leaves off the element of time. C and D are wordy. You will practice more of this type of editing for clarity and style in the Writing Processes chapter.

Writing Processes/ part 15

4. **(A)** This question will seem easy after question 5, especially since you have been proofreading your own writing for years. When you first read through the draft paragraph, I bet you noticed the errors in sentences 1 and 3 automatically. C and D are poor choices because of "me." "I" is the correct pronoun to use as the subject. Between A and B, A is the better choice.

Writing Processes/ part 15

5. **(B)** This sentence includes the double negative, "had not hardly." The only way to correct this is to remove the negative "not." Because A is a run-on, choice B is the best answer.

Writing Processes/ part 9

6. **(B)** Writing for an audience is a crucial skill in the entire test, as it will be a part of your written responses to the long and short answer questions as well as ones like this one. For an elementary school audience, you will need to simply the length of your sentences and to make the vocabulary less scientific and

sophisticated. But you must not lose the essence of the sample sentence. Choice B is the one that does all of this. C and D are overly complicated, and A is too specific, losing its closeness to the main idea in the sample sentence.

Writing Processes/ part 13

7. **(A)** This is a mix between proofreading and editing. The errors in the draft paragraph are serious but not necessarily as obvious as in questions 4 and 5. Sample sentence 2 has a misplaced modifier. It sounds as if the sky is looking up rather than the speaker. Choice A is the only one that corrects that error without adding other issues such as wordiness or unclear and complicated writing.

Writing Processes/ part 15

8. **(A)** This error involving possessive apostrophes should have been more obvious. We assume that "friends" is plural, and because of that, the apostrophe should go outside the "s." Choice A is the only one to correctly accomplish this.

Writing Processes/ part 14

9. **(C)** These questions may look complicated, but if you think about it, they actually give you all that you need to know right in the question. The comma rules are presented. And then in the sample sentence, you have an example of one of the types of rules—the use of two adjectives to describe the same noun. The only choice that correctly punctuates that without adding other errors is choice C. The other choice, B, that has the correct comma between the adjectives "long" and "rainy" adds other commas where it should not, according to the rules presented.

Writing Processes/ part 12

10. **(C)** This question is really just asking you if you know what types of resources to use and when—and I bet you do, since you have been using them in school and at home for years. Since a dictionary and a thesaurus are for the use of words, we can eliminate them. You may find a geologist to interview, but that would be going above and beyond the assignment. While there's nothing wrong with that, choice C, "atlas," which would involve maps is the better choice. You would simply have to include some sort of maps in a paper about the movement over time of glaciers in North America.

So how did you do? You may have noticed that all of the diagnostic questions are about Writing Processes, all of which are discussed and practiced in Chapter 8. The reason is simple — most of the multiple-choice questions on the Writing OGT are about Writing Processes. We will discuss and practice Writing Applications and Writing Conventions later, as well as practice scoring your best on the short essay and extended response questions. Before you dive into Chapter 1, take some time to analyze any areas that concern you, so that you can put extra energy and focus into those items when you see them during the course of going through the many chapters in the book.

It's time to begin your study and practice. Keep in mind what Coach K of Duke University once said: "Confidence shared is better than confidence only in yourself." Remember that all of those around you have confidence in the levels of success you will be able to achieve with this resource, their support, and your own hard work and focus.

PART 1

THE READING OGT

An Overview—What's on the Reading OGT?

In the State of Ohio there are many academic content standards in English/Language Arts; however, you will only be asked to show competency in some of them.

THE STANDARDS TESTED ON THE READING OGT

The first standard is Acquisition of Vocabulary. This is just like it sounds, and you can even test your potential by looking at its name. *Acquire* is the root of the word *acquisition*, which means "to obtain" or "to get." And you certainly know what "vocabulary" means. Simply put, this standard is all about how you know what a word means, including roots, prefixes, suffixes, context clues, and other relationships between the word in question and the words around it. Sound like a lot? It might be, but remember two things. First, you use these concepts all the time without even knowing it. Second, you'll jump right into practicing this in Chapter 2.

The second academic content standard on the Reading OGT is Reading Process: Concepts of Print, Comprehension Strategies, and Self-Monitoring Strategies. That's a mouthful, but like the previous standard, you do it all the time! This one involves making predictions, summarizing, making inferences, and drawing conclusions. Any time you read a book, even for pleasure, you do all of those things.

Third is the standard for Reading Applications: Informational, Technical, and Persuasive Text. You can use that Acquisition of Vocabulary skill to figure out what this one means. You will be asked to analyze informational texts, such as nonfiction. You may also be asked questions about something technical, such as a scientific journal or chart. And, you must be able to analyze the techniques of persuasion, otherwise known as rhetoric.

Finally, you must navigate the fourth content standard of Reading Applications: Literary Text. This is what all great English classes are made of. It includes skills such as identifying an author's use of characterization, point of view, foreshadowing, flashback—all the biggies. There's also some mood, tone, irony, and figurative language in there for good measure.

WHAT THE ACTUAL TEST LOOKS LIKE

The test will have 38 test questions, with six that are being field-tested for future use, meaning they won't be part of your score. You won't know which ones they are, so always do your best. A closer look at the test shows that the test will have 32 multiple-choice items, four short-answer questions, and two extended-response questions. There will be a total of five passages to read, three of which will be on Informational Text, and two on Literary Text. Finally, of those passages, there are two short (under 500 words), two medium (500–900 words), and two long (900–1200 words).

The short-answer questions are scored using a 2-point scale or rubric; the extended responses are scored using a 4-point scale or rubric.

HOW THE TEST IS SCORED

The multiple-choice test questions are worth 32 points, short-answer questions are worth 8 points, and extended-response questions are worth 8 points. The total points available on the test are 48. Your tests are scored by highly trained outside contractors, who are provided with scoring guides and rubrics created by teachers from all over the state of Ohio.

The Five Score Ranges

For the March 2005 administration of the Reading OGT, the following ranges were applied to the students' test results. These ranges are based on the "cut scores" decided upon by the Ohio State Board of Education, as recommended by the Range-finding Committee, comprised of Ohio teachers.

	Raw Score	Scaled Score
Advanced	40.0–48.0	448–545
Accelerated	32.0–39.5	429–447
Proficient	18.0–31.5	400–428
—————————————passing line—————————————		
Basic	12.0–17.5	383–399
Limited	0.0–11.5	268–382

Students sometimes wonder if the test is easy to pass, and how much more difficult it is to score in the accelerated and advanced sections. It is important to remember that the cut scores, or different levels, can change each year, based on the decisions of the State Board of Education. Also, each year the reading passages and questions change, so it is difficult to estimate how a student will do. The best advice is simply to do your best and to do everything you can to reach your full potential.

Acquisition of Vocabulary

The Reading OGT will derive 8–9 of the 48 points from this standard, mostly in the form of multiple-choice questions.

Looking over the standard, note that many of the concepts are part of your everyday classes, if not your everyday life. Any time you read something, you may have to find out what a word means by using context clues or other tricks of the trade. Also note that point number 6 of this standard is unlikely to be part of the OGT because it requires outside knowledge and outside resources. Numbers 1–5 are the keys, and you will soon learn how to make sure you get every single one of them correct on the test.

The Standard in Action

So, you see a group of words together, and they start with a capital letter and end with a period. What is this called? I bet you know, but if you didn't, you could simply look at what I have just said about it and—there's your answer. It's a sentence. That's using the context.

You may also be asked to select an antonym (the opposite of the word provided) or a synonym a word similar in meaning to the one provided. Part of this will be easier using the process of elimination, which will be discussed later when we handle test-taking skills.

Finally, the figurative language questions on the test will be *as easy as pie*. You see the simile I just used, right? I used "like" or "as" to compare taking the test to "pie."

What the Standard Looks Like on the Actual OGT

All this talk about standards and what it is in real life is all well and good, but you probably want to see how it might look on the actual OGT. For the Acquisition of Vocabulary standard, the questions will look like the following, modeled after previous versions of the Reading OGT. They all follow a reading passage.

EXAMPLE 1

You will be given a sentence from the passage and asked a question, such as:

In the excerpt from the passage, the word <u>prosperity</u> means

A. success.
B. power.
C. wealth.
D. fame.

You may be tempted simply to look at the underlined word and find the most obvious meaning from the choices, but be careful. It is important for you to go back and reread the sentence and word in its context. This may be a word that has several meanings, like *pool*, and you will not be able just to use your previous knowledge of the word. Always look back at the passage when they give you an excerpt.

EXAMPLE 2

You will be given a sentence from the passage and asked a question, such as the following:

Which definition represents the intended meaning of the word <u>missing</u>?

A. failing to hit
B. discovering the absence of
C. failing to obtain
D. leaving out

Look familiar? It should, because this is the same question asked in a different way; the choices are all definitions for the word "missing." You still must find the word in its original context in the passage to be certain of the correct definition, just like last time. In this case, each of the answer choices is reasonable, so you absolutely must go back to guarantee the correct answer. It's worth the time to make sure you earn the point!

EXAMPLE 3

You will be given a sentence from the passage and asked a question, such as:

Which word represents the meaning of <u>articulated</u>?

A. talked to
B. explained
C. mumbled
D. written to

Once again, you are being given the same type of question but in a different manner. You still have to read the choices and verify your answer by looking back at the passage for the proper context.

EXAMPLE 4

You will be given a sentence from the passage and asked a question, such as:

According to the information given in the passage, the prefix *sub*, as in <u>submarine</u>, must refer to

A. something after the water.
B. something below the water.
C. something on top of the water.
D. something without water.

EXAMPLE 5

You will be given a sentence from the passage and asked a question, such as the following:

As used in paragraph two, a <u>carpenter</u> is one who

A. makes carpet.
B. works with wood.
C. makes houses.
D. works with metal.

This question is basically the same as the others. You're probably getting the hang of it now. But here's one that is different.

EXAMPLE 6

You may be given a passage that discusses something about our language and how certain words were formed, or how they became a part of the English language. This will be in the form of a short-answer question worth 2 points. You will use evidence from the passage to support your answer, but the actual answer will be in the passage for you to find. We will discuss how to score well on short-answer questions later.

TIPS FOR ANSWERING VOCABULARY QUESTIONS, ESPECIALLY THE TRICKY ONES

The best tip is to read carefully and discipline yourself to go back to the passage to verify the correct answer. Don't assume that since you recognize the word and see its match in the answer choices that that's the correct choice. It's always worth your time to go back to be positive.

The good news about preparing to tackle this section is that these types of questions also appear on the PSAT, ACT, and SAT. And in those cases, you can bet that they will try to trick you. There will be words on these tests that have a simple and common definition, which will be put as answer choice A. But that won't be how the word in question is used in the passage! You can just guess what happens much of the time—a student in a hurry selects the quick and easy answer without looking back at the passage. It's not the end of the world, but there is no reason to miss these questions.

So, are you ready to try a couple? Let's see how you do. First, read the passage below from a *Time* magazine article.

Debacle on Ice: Like Many American Athletes in Torino, NHLers Fume After Loss

At least we beat Kazakhstan. The U.S. hockey team's <u>bid</u> for a medal flittered away Wednesday night in the quarterfinals against Finland, just like the puck scampering between U.S. goalie Rick DiPietro's legs. The U.S. had a single win in six games, against Kazakhstan, and a tie against Latvia, another Soviet hockey stepchild. On the 26th anniversary of the USA's Miracle on Ice win over the Soviet Union in Lake Placid, NY, the only miracle Wednesday night was that the U.S. actually showed some energy at the end of the game, losing by a single goal, 4–3. And that the coach and star player didn't exchange body <u>checks</u>.

Okay, let's see if you have this standard mastered.

Question 1

According to the passage, the word <u>bid</u> means

A. to offer money for.
B. an attempt.
C. to invite.
D. an invitation.

One thing to note is that in the choices there are two verbs, A and C, and two nouns, B and D. Once you find the word *bid* in the passage, you'll see that it's used as a noun. You will want to choose the answer showing the part of speech that matches the use. That leaves choices B and D. Going back to the word as used in the passage, "the U.S. hockey team's bid for a medal," choice B, meaning "an attempt," is the clear winner.

Let's try another one.

Question 2

"And that the coach and star player didn't exchange body <u>checks</u>."

Which word means the same as the word <u>checks</u>?

A. methods of payment
B. marks used to keep track of something
C. violently running into another person
D. to leave for safekeeping

If you look this word up in the passage, even though the excerpt is provided for you, you will see that the only logical answer is C. The other three answers don't fit the context of a hockey game. Even though you *might* have gotten it right using the excerpt only, make sure you go back and check the passage to be sure.

Let's go through more sample items on the Acquisition of Vocabulary standards and see if these examples have paid off.

Read the following passage from George Orwell's *Animal Farm*:

At one end of the big barn, on a sort of raised platform, Major was already ensconced on his bed of straw, under a lantern which hung from a beam. He was twelve years old and had lately grown rather <u>stout</u>, but he was still a majestic-looking pig, with a wise and <u>benevolent</u> appearance in spite of the fact that his tushes had never been cut. Before long the other animals began to arrive and make themselves <u>comfortable</u> after their different fashions. First came the three dogs, Bluebell, Jessie, and Pincher, and then the pigs, who settled down in the straw immediately in front of the platform. The hens perched themselves on the window-sills, the pigeons fluttered up to the rafters, the sheep and cows lay down behind the pigs and began to chew the cud. The two cart-horses, Boxer and Clover, came in together, walking very slowly and setting down their vast hairy hoofs with great care lest there should be some small animal concealed in the straw. Clover was a stout motherly mare approaching middle life, who had never quite got her figure back after her fourth foal. Boxer was an enormous beast, nearly eighteen hands high, and as strong as any two ordinary horses put together. A white stripe down his nose gave him a somewhat stupid appearance, and in fact he was not of first-rate intelligence, but he was <u>universally</u> respected for his steadiness of character and tremendous powers of work. After the horses came Muriel, the white goat, and Benjamin, the donkey. Benjamin was the oldest animal on the farm, and the worst tempered. He seldom talked, and when he did, it was usually to make some cynical remark-for instance, he would say that God had given him a tail to keep the flies off, but that he would sooner have had no tail and no flies. Alone among the animals on the farm he never laughed. If asked why, he would say that he saw nothing to laugh at. Nevertheless, without openly admitting it, he was devoted to Boxer; the two of them usually spent their Sundays together in the small paddock beyond the orchard, grazing side by side and never speaking.

The two horses had just lain down when a <u>brood</u> of ducklings, which had lost their mother, <u>filed</u> into the barn, cheeping feebly and wandering from side to side to find some place where they would not be trodden on. Clover made a sort of wall round them with her great foreleg, and the ducklings nestled down inside it and promptly fell asleep. At the last moment Mollie, the foolish, pretty white mare who drew Mr. Jones's trap, came mincing daintily in, chewing at a lump of sugar. She took a place near the front and began flirting her white mane, hoping to draw attention to the red ribbons it was plaited with. Last of all came the cat, who looked round, as usual, for the warmest place, and finally squeezed herself in between Boxer and Clover; there she purred <u>contentedly</u> throughout Major's speech without listening to a word of what he was saying.

Using Context Clues

Question 3

"He was twelve years old and had lately grown rather <u>stout</u>, but he was still a majestic-looking pig, with a wise and benevolent appearance . . . ."

Which word represents the intended meaning of <u>stout</u>?

A. happy
B. angry
C. large
D. satisfied

In this case, we see that Major is getting older, and the word "stout" is preceded by the word grown. When we consider the rest of the sentence, it is clear that C, "large," is the best answer.

Question 4

"Last of all came the cat, who looked round, as usual, for the warmest place, and finally squeezed herself in between Boxer and Clover; there she purred <u>contentedly</u> . . . ."

Which word represents the opposite of the word <u>contentedly</u>?

A. in a satisfied way
B. in joyful way
C. in a disruptive way
D. in a pleased way

Did you read the question carefully? If so, this was an easy one. The only choice that is even close to an opposite of "contentedly" is C, "in a disruptive way." If you didn't read the question carefully, you should have really struggled, unless you simply chose the first one that looked close, A. Always read all of the choices before selecting an answer.

Question 5

As used in the passage, <u>filed</u> means

A. arranged in order.
B. marched.
C. rubbed smooth.
D. placed among official records.

In this case, it is important to go back to the passage and be sure of how the word is being used in context, especially a common word such as filed. If you were to return to the passage here, you would read the following sentence:

> "The two horses had just lain down when a brood of ducklings,
> which had lost their mother, filed into the barn . . . ."

This helps us to see that this verb has to do with the ducklings moving into the barn, which means that the only logical answer is B, "to march." Let's do another one in that same sentence.

Question 6

According to the passage, <u>brood</u> means

A. to ponder.
B. to worry.
C. a common group.
D. kept for breeding.

In the passage, the word "brood" is used to refer to the group of ducklings, so C looks like the best answer. If you take a closer look, you will see that C is also the only word that is a noun, which means that the others are of parts of speech that don't match how "brood" is used in the passage. "To ponder," and "to worry," are infinitives, or forms of verbs. "Kept for breeding" is an adjective phrase. Whenever you can, try to think through each answer so that you are sure it is correct.

Using Prefixes, Suffixes, and Roots

Let's look at some prefixes before we do more practice. Take a look at the following prefix chart showing their definitions. The most common ones have been left blank—try to fill them in as you review. Cover the bottom half of the page so you don't see the answers before you've had a chance to try them.

a not	**co** _____	**hemi** half
mid _____	**per** throughout	**tele** far
ab away from	**com** with	**hyper** above, over
mini _____	**poly** _____	**trans** across, over
anti _____	**con** with	**il/im** not
mis wrong	**port** carry	**tri** _____
auto _____	**contra** against	**in/ir** not
mono _____	**post** _____	**ultra** beyond
bene good	**pre** _____	**inter** _____
multi _____	**pro** _____	**un** not, uncertain
bi _____	**dia** through	**magni** great, large
non not	**quad** _____	**under** _____
bio _____	**dis** apart	**mega** great
over too much	**re** _____	**uni** _____
cent hundred	**semi** _____	**ex** not, out of
pan all	**equi** equal	**super** above
para beside, guard	**sub** _____	**penta** five
circum around		

How did you do? Here are the answers to the blank ones, so that you can check your accuracy:

mid—half	quad—four	co—with, together
bi—two, double	under—below	mini—very small
re—again, back	uni—one, all	poly—many
anti—against	semi—half, partly	post—after
auto—self, alone	sub—below, under	pre—before
mono—one, single	tri—three	multi—many
pro—forward, supporting	inter—between, among	bio—life

Now let's try a few sample questions for which you must use your knowledge of prefixes. We will use the same passage from *Animal Farm*.

Question 7

"He was twelve years old and had lately grown rather stout, but he was still a majestic-looking pig, with a wise and <u>benevolent</u> appearance . . . ."

The word <u>benevolent</u> means

A. smart.
B. likely to do good.
C. violent.
D. ruffled.

In this question, the context is not obvious enough to give you the answer. You should notice that the word "benevolent" has the prefix *bene*. Check back on the list, and you will see that *bene* means "good." This makes B, "likely to do good," the only possible answer.

Question 8

In the passage, the narrator states that Boxer was "<u>universally</u> respected for his steadiness of character and tremendous powers of work."

Which definition represents the intended meaning of the word <u>universally</u>?

A. implying every member
B. referring to the universe
C. referring to a small amount
D. implying only the self

Examine the prefix <u>uni</u> in this word, which means "one." Note that <u>uni</u> is also used to refer to "all" or "all working as a group." Also, if you look at the broader context of the sentence, it is clear that all of the animals feel the same about Boxer. In this case, A, "implying every member," is the best answer.

Now let's look at some of the most common suffixes that are important for you to know.

SUFFIXES THAT CREATE NOUNS

ity—condition or quality of (flexibil<u>ity</u>)
ment—state or result of   (content<u>ment</u>)
sion, tion—act of (frustra<u>tion</u>)
ness—state of (happi<u>ness</u>)
ance, ence—act, state, quality of (assist<u>ance</u>)
er, or, ist—one who does (compos<u>er</u>)

SUFFIXES THAT CREATE ADJECTIVES

ive—tending toward doing some action (fest<u>ive</u>)
y—having (rain<u>y</u>)
able—can (port<u>able</u>)
en—made of (wood<u>en</u>)
less—without (power<u>less</u>)
ous—having or full of (mysteri<u>ous</u>)
ic—characteristic of (hero<u>ic</u>)
al—relating to (financi<u>al</u>)
ful—having or full of (wonder<u>ful</u>)

Question 9

In the sentence, "Before long, the other animals began to arrive and make themselves <u>comfortable</u> after their different fashions," what is the intended meaning of the word <u>comfortable</u>?

A. uneasiness
B. with physical comfort
C. resting
D. sleepiness

In this example, knowing that the suffix *able* creates an adjective can help you find the right answer. "Uneasiness" ends in a suffix and creates a noun. "Resting" is a verb, and "sleepiness" is also a noun. This makes B, "with physical comfort" the only correct answer.

And finally, let's look at some important roots for you to know.

Greek Root	Meaning	Example
anthrop	human	anthropology
chron	time	synchronize
dem	people	democracy
morph	form	metamorphic
path	feeling, suffering	sympathy, apathy
pedo/ped	child, children	pediatrician
philo/phil	having a strong affinity or love for	philosophy
phon	sound	phonetics

Latin Root	Meaning	Example
dict	to say	contradict, dictate
duc	to lead, bring, take	produce, reduce
gress	to walk	progress
ject	to throw	eject, inject, reject
pel	to drive	compel, repel
pend	to hang	pendant, pendulum
port	to carry	export, import
scrib/script	to write	describe, prescribe
tract	to pull, drag, draw	attract, extract, retract
vert	to turn	convert, invert

Now try a few questions that combine your knowledge of prefixes, suffixes, and roots.

Question 10

"At the beginning they met with much stupidity and <u>apathy</u>."

Which of the following shows the intended meaning of the word <u>apathy</u>?

A. thoughtfulness
B. anger
C. sadness
D. lack of caring

Here, you can see that the root *path* refers to "caring." Also, you will remember that the prefix *a* means "not." If you put those two together, you have "not caring," which is a nice match to the correct answer, D, lack of caring.

Question 11

"And so, almost before they knew what was happening, the Rebellion had been successfully carried through: Jones was <u>expelled</u>, and the Manor Farm was theirs."

Which of the following is the opposite of the word <u>expelled</u>?

A. thrown out
B. asked to change
C. invited in
D. ignored

This is another example where your combined knowledge of prefixes and roots will help. You can see that *ex* means "out of." And, you know that *pel* means "to drive." So, choice A, "thrown out," must be correct, right? Be careful! If you look closely at the question, you'll see that it asks for the opposite, making C, invited in, the correct answer.

Question 12

"These Seven Commandments would now be <u>inscribed</u> on the wall; they would form an unalterable law by which all the animals on Animal Farm must live for ever after."

What word represents the meaning of the word <u>inscribed</u>?

A. written or printed upon
B. given to
C. imagined
D. told to

The prefix *scribe* means "to write," so for this one it's clear to see that A, "written or printed upon," is the best choice. That even fits in well using the basic "plug in for context clues." If you read the sentence and insert "written" for "inscribed," it works well, too.

So far, we have reviewed and practiced context clues and word pairs such as synonyms and antonyms. We have also discussed prefixes, suffixes, and roots and how they can help you understand unknown words. Next we will look at metaphors, similes, idioms, and puns.

Metaphors, Similes, Idioms, and Puns

Let's start off with the basic definitions.

metaphor: a direct comparison

simile: a comparison using "like" or "as"

idiom: an expression unique to a certain people

pun: humorous use of a word that suggests two meanings

Here's what they look like in action.

METAPHOR

". . . Juliet is the sun."

In this example from Shakespeare's *Romeo and Juliet*, Romeo sees Juliet appear on her balcony and says, "But soft, what light through yonder window breaks? It is the East, and Juliet is the sun." He attempts to praise her beauty and brightness by comparing her to the sun.

SIMILE

Juliet is like the sun.

Here is the same example, only it uses "like" rather than simply saying that Juliet *is* the sun. That small difference is all that separates similes from metaphors.

IDIOM

Close, but no cigar.

This expression is used to imply that you are close to success but are still experiencing the disappointment of failure. This expression comes from the time when cigars were given out as prizes in slot machines or at carnivals. What makes this an idiom is that it is not likely that it would be easy for someone from another country to understand how this expression is used, and if this were translated directly, it might have an odd or humorous meaning in another language. Idioms are not meant to be taken literally.

PUN

My biologist friend tells me that constantly developing new varieties of plants can be a strain.

Here we have a pun using the word *strain*. We know that *strain* is used here to mean "strong effort," but it becomes a play on the meaning of the word in its scientific sense, meaning "group."

Let's practice identifying these.

Directions: After each example below, write in the name of which of the four elements you think it represents.

1. He laughed his head off. _____

2. Old kings never die; they just get throne away. _____

3. The salesman was a shark. _____

4. Clouds are like marshmallows in the sky. _____

Let's see how you did. The first expression, which is an exaggeration used to show that something is extremely funny, is an idiom. It is likely that someone who is just learning English would not understand that this is not meant to be taken literally. The second one uses the word *throne* rather than the word *thrown*. This is a pun because the sentence is about a king, which makes the similar-sounding word amusing. The third example compares a salesman to a shark directly, making it a metaphor. Finally, because the fourth one uses "like" to compare the clouds to marshmallows, it is a simile.

See if you can make your own sentences using the four elements discussed above:

Idiom: _____

Pun: _____

Metaphor: _____

Simile: _____

A DIFFERENT TWIST ON ACQUISITION OF VOCABULARY

One of the standards that is not as common but still appears in the area of Acquisition of Vocabulary is to "understand and analyze ways that historical events have influenced the English language. Read the following article, paying close attention to the reasons given for how our language changed and developed:

Standardization

The late medieval and early modern periods saw a fairly steady process of standardization in English south of the Scottish border. The written and spoken language of London continued to evolve and gradually began to have a greater influence in the country at large. For most of the Middle English period a dialect was simply what was spoken in a particular area, which would normally be more or less represented in writing—although where and from whom the writer had learnt how to write were also important. It was only when the broadly London standard began to dominate, especially through the new technology of printing, that the other regional varieties of the language began to be seen as different in kind.

In the same period a series of changes also occurred in English pronunciation (though not uniformly in all dialects), which go under the collective name of the Great Vowel Shift. These were purely linguistic 'sound changes' which occur in every language in every period of history. The changes in pronunciation weren't the result of specific social or historical factors, but social and historical factors would have helped to spread the results of the changes. As a result the so-called 'pure' vowel sounds which still characterize many continental languages were lost to English. The phonetic pairings of most long and short vowel sounds were also lost, which gave rise to many of the oddities of English pronunciation, and which now obscure the relationships between many English words and their foreign counterparts.

Colonization and Globalization

During the medieval and early modern periods the influence of English spread throughout the British Isles, and from the early seventeenth century onwards its influence began to be felt throughout the world. The complex processes of exploration, colonization and overseas trade that characterized Britain's external relations for several centuries became agents for change in the English language. This wasn't simply through the acquisition of loan-words deriving from languages from every corner of the world, which in many cases only entered English via the languages of other trading and imperial nations such as Spain, Portugal and the Netherlands, but through the gradual development of new varieties of English, each with their own nuances of vocabulary and grammar and their own distinct pronunciations. More recently still, English has become a . . . global language, regularly used and understood by many nations for whom English is not their first language. The eventual effects on the English language of both of these developments can only be guessed at today, but there can be little doubt that they will be as important as anything that has happened to English in the past sixteen hundred years.

(http://www.askoxford.com/worldofwords/history/?view=uk)

According to the article, which events influenced our language, and how did they influence our language? Make a list of any details from the article that you would use to answer the question:

_____

_____

_____

_____

_____

Let's see how you did. Here are the key details from the passage:

- The written and spoken language of London continued to evolve and gradually began to have a greater influence in the country at large.

- It was only when the broadly London standard began to dominate, especially through the new technology of printing, that the other regional varieties of the language began to be seen as different in kind.

- The changes in pronunciation weren't the result of specific social or historical factors, but social and historical factors would have helped to spread the results of the changes.

- The complex processes of exploration, colonization, and overseas trade that characterized Britain's external relations for several centuries became agents for change in the English language.

If you are asked to respond to a question like this on the Reading OGT, it will come with a passage to read like this practice one. You will also likely be asked to respond in short-answer or extended-response form, which we will discuss later.

Another part of the Acquisition of Vocabulary standard that is uncommon but worth practicing involves "using dictionaries, thesauruses, glossaries, technology and textual features, such as definitional footnotes or sidebars." Let's make sure you can answer questions about those items if asked to on the Reading OGT.

Dictionary Entry

The following is the dictionary entry for the word *pool* from the *Merriam Webster's Online Dictionary*:

[1]pool
Pronunciation: 'pü (&) l
Function: *noun*
Etymology: Middle English, from Old English *pOl;* akin to Old High German *pfuol* pool 1 a (1) : a small and rather deep body of usually fresh water (2) : a quiet place in a stream (3) : a body of water forming above a dam b : something resembling a pool <a *pool* of light>
2 : a small body of standing liquid
3 : a continuous area of porous sedimentary rock that yields petroleum or gas
4 : <u>SWIMMING POOL</u>
[2]pool
Function: *intransitive verb*
1 : to form a pool
2 *of blood* : to accumulate or become static (as in the veins of a bodily part)

According to the information given, you can see that the word is from Middle English, as explained in the "Etymology" section. It also has two main definitions, one of which is a noun, and the other is a verb. Each of those has different versions of the definition, as well. You may be asked to answer a question about a certain definition, and you will need to be able to read the entry and find the correct part of speech as well as the correct definition as it fits the example.

For instance, if you were asked to choose the entry that matches the use of *pool* in the following sentence, which one would you choose?

We played volleyball in the pool.

Here are your choices from above:

A. a small and rather deep body of usually fresh water; a quiet place in a stream; a body of water forming above a dam

B. a small body of standing liquid
C. a continuous area of porous sedimentary rock that yields petroleum or gas
D. swimming pool
E. to form a pool
F. to accumulate or become static

It will help you if you remember that in the sample sentence, *pool* is used as a noun, so choices E and F, as verbs, are not possible answers. That means that D, "swimming pool," is the best fit. Remember, all you needed to do to answer that correctly was to read the sample sentence and find the best fit from the definitions provided in the dictionary entry. However, first it was necessary to know how to read and understand how the entry was organized in the dictionary.

Here's another example:

Main Entry: ¹chance
Pronunciation: 'chan(t)s
Function: *noun*
Etymology: Middle English, from Old French, from (assumed) Vulgar Latin *cadentia* fall, from Latin *cadent-, cadens,* present participle of *cadere* to fall; perhaps akin to Sanskrit *sad-* to fall off

1 a : something that happens unpredictably without discernible human intention or observable cause b : the assumed impersonal purposeless determiner of unaccountable happenings
2 : opportunity
3 : a fielding opportunity in baseball
4 : the possibility of a particular outcome in an uncertain situation; *also* : the degree of likelihood of such an outcome
5 : risk

Let's see how you do on matching these sample sentences.

> **Directions:** Fill in the blanks using the number of the definition as your choice:

_____ She took a chance and called him.

_____ It was a once-in-a-lifetime chance.

_____ They felt that the events of their life all happened by chance.

_____ Chances were that they had already left.

Based on the information provided in the dictionary entry, here's how you should have answered. The first one involves a risk, so the correct answer is 5. The second sentence refers to an opportunity, making the correct answer 2. The third example refers to unpredictability, so the correct answer is 1. Finally, the last sentence refers to the possibility of an outcome, making the correct answer 4.

When it comes to this type of question, you will do well if you take your time and read the entry carefully.

Thesaurus Entry

Reading a thesaurus entry is similar to reading that of a dictionary. In fact, it may be easier because it will not have as much information. The purpose of a thesaurus is to allow the user to find different words that have the same meaning or opposite meanings. In the entry below, you can see that it is important to make sure that the parts of speech match. Also, note where the entry switches to "antonyms," or opposites.

Entry Word: chance
Function: *noun*
Synonyms: accident, circumstance, hap, hazard, luck
Related Words: fortuitousness, randomness, uncertainty; fluke; destiny, doom, fate, fortune, lot; danger, peril, risk
OPPORTUNITY
PROBABILITY
GAMBLE
Near Antonyms: intent, intention, purpose; design, outline, plan, scheme

In this entry, you may be asked to select a "synonym" or a similar word. Your choices in this case are *accident, circumstance, hap, hazard, luck, opportunity, probability,* or *gamble.* You must make sure that you choose the one that matches the context of the sample sentence, much like you did with the dictionary entry. They are not interchangeable. For example:

She took a gamble and called him.

It was a once-in-a-lifetime opportunity.

They felt that the events of their life all happened by luck.

Probability was that they had already left.

Glossaries

A glossary by definition is a "list of brief explanations." You must be able to navigate this much like you did the dictionary and thesaurus entries. Here is a sample glossary:

GLOSSARY OF POETRY TERMS

accent The prominence or emphasis given to a syllable or word. In the word *poetry*, the accent (or stress) falls on the first syllable.

alliteration The repetition of the same or similar sounds at the beginning of words: "What would the world be, once bereft/Of wet and wildness?" (Gerard Manley Hopkins, "Inversnaid")

anapest A metrical foot of three syllables, two short (or unstressed) followed by one long (or stressed), as in *seventeen* and *to the moon.* The anapest is the reverse of the dactyl.

antithesis A figure of speech in which words and phrases with opposite meanings are balanced against each other. An example of antithesis is "To err is human, to forgive, divine." (Alexander Pope)

apostrophe Words that are spoken to a person who is absent or imaginary, or to an object or abstract idea. The poem "God's World" by Edna St. Vincent Millay begins with an apostrophe: "O World, I cannot hold thee close enough!/Thy winds, thy wide grey skies!/Thy mists that roll and rise!"

assonance   The repetition or a pattern of similar sounds, especially vowel sounds: "Thou still unravished bride of quietness,/Thou foster child of silence and slow time" ("Ode to a Grecian Urn," John Keats).

ballad   A poem that tells a story similar to a folk tale or legend and often has a repeated refrain. "The Rime of the Ancient Mariner" by Samuel Taylor Coleridge is an example of a ballad.

ballade   A type of poem, usually with three stanzas of seven, eight, or ten lines and a shorter final stanza (or envoy) of four or five lines. All stanzas end with the same one-line refrain.

blank verse   Poetry that is written in unrhymed iambic pentameter. Shakespeare wrote most of his plays in blank verse.

caesura   A natural pause or break in a line of poetry, usually near the middle of the line. There is a caesura right after the question mark in the first line of this sonnet by Elizabeth Barrett Browning: "How do I love thee? Let me count the ways."

canzone   A medieval Italian lyric poem, with five or six stanzas and a shorter concluding stanza (or envoy). The poets Petrarch and Dante Alighieri were masters of the canzone.

carpe diem   A Latin expression that means "seize the day." Carpe diem poems urge the reader (or the person to whom they are addressed) to live for today and enjoy the pleasures of the moment. A famous carpe diem poem by Robert Herrick begins "Gather ye rosebuds while ye may . . ."

(http://www.infoplease.com/ipa/A0903237.html)

This is only a small part of the entire glossary, but it's enough to illustrate how to use it. You will notice that it's arranged alphabetically, and each entry includes a definition and an example. You may be asked to answer a question that requires you to find something that is in the glossary, but it might not simply be the main entry.

For example, what is the poetic term for "a natural break or pause"? You may not know from memory, and you can't simply find the answer by looking at the main entry word. But because you know that glossaries have definitions, you can find the answer to the question—"caesura."

Footnotes

Just like the name says, a footnote is a note of reference at the bottom of a page. These are easy to find, and if the writer has taken the time to put information in a footnote, you can bet it's important and worth reading.

In this description of the purpose of footnotes, there is an indication after the first sentence, using the superscript [1], that the reader should check the bottom of the page for more information. This could have easily been the answer to the question, "Why are footnotes necessary?" This information is not contained in the actual passage, but is easily found in the footnote.

footnotes   Any information considered vital to the proper understanding of the story should be in the text and not buried in the footnotes.[1] Keep information footnotes for cross-referencing purposes to a minimum. Footnotes may, however, be used when there is a need to inform the reader that a certain important subject will be covered in later pages or to remind the reader it has already been examined.

[1]The writer can use information or explanatory footnotes, however, to improve the flow of the narrative by removing nonessential but pertinent material from the text, while providing it to the reader.

(from http://www.tecom.usmc.mil/HD/PDF_Files/MCHC%20Writing%20Guide.pdf)

Chapter 2 Wrap-Up

This chapter was about the content standard for Acquisition of Vocabulary. You have seen the standard as it appears in its official form. Also, you have seen examples and sample questions much like you will see on the Reading OGT. Later, you will get a chance to practice these as they appear as part of a larger test involving all of the standards, but don't leave this chapter without reviewing the major concepts:

- There are many ways to find the correct answers when it comes to questions about definitions and meanings of words. In nearly every case, you have to take your time and make sure you understand the context of the passage.

- You most likely already know many prefixes, roots, and suffixes, and can use that knowledge to help you find the correct answers.

- To answer these types of questions correctly, you will call upon common test-taking skills that you have been developing for years, such as process of elimination and plugging in the right answer. Plus, we will review those strategies before you take the practice tests in this book.

Now let's move on to Reading Process: Concepts of Print, Comprehension Strategies, and Self-Monitoring Strategies.

Reading Process: Concepts of Print, Comprehension Strategies, and Self-Monitoring Strategies

THE STANDARD

1. Apply reading comprehension strategies, including making predictions, comparing and contrasting, recalling and summarizing and making inferences and drawing conclusions.
2. Answer literal, inferential, evaluative and synthesizing questions to demonstrate comprehension of grade-appropriate print texts and electronic and visual media.
3. Monitor own comprehension by adjusting speed to fit the purpose, or by skimming, scanning, reading on, looking back, note taking or summarizing what has been read so far in text.
4. Use criteria to choose independent reading materials (e.g., personal interest, knowledge of authors and genres or recommendations from others).
5. Independently read books for various purposes (e.g., for enjoyment, for literary experience, to gain information or to perform a task).

The Reading OGT will derive 10–16 of the 48 points from this standard, mostly in the form of multiple-choice questions.

This standard is what we might call the "meat and potatoes" of reading for an English class. It's all about your ability to read and comprehend a text. Parts 1 and 2 are the essence of the standard. Parts 3, 4, and 5 are important but not likely to appear on the OGT, as they are difficult to "test."

The Standard in Action

You may be asked the main idea of a passage in this standard, and it might be phrased as simply as, "this passage is about" or "why" does something happen. You may even be asked something as basic as a question about the events that occurred in a passage. This type of detail question is typically attractive, because the answer is sitting right in the passage for you to find.

Another way you'll see this standard appear is by being asked to paraphrase a statement from the passage. To paraphrase is to say something in a different way but still keep the same meaning.

Also, the questions for this standard might be phrased as "what point is the author making?" or "what is the author's purpose?"

The thing to keep in mind is that this standard is made up of skills that you have worked on in English class for years. You will want to relax and read, trusting that you are going to be able to find the answers to these questions if you take your time and think.

What the Standard Looks Like on the Actual OGT

You will be given a reading passage of fiction, nonfiction, or poetry to go along with the types of questions discussed above. The questions will likely be multiple choice, but they may also ask you a short-answer question.

Consider the short passage below to use with the following sample questions:

Kylie-Ayn Kennedy, 16, likes to get to the tanning parlor first thing in the morning. "The beds are cooler," explains the honor student in Easton, Pa. "By the end of the day, they're really hot when you get into them. After five minutes, you're sweating to death." So Kennedy, who has a summer job waitressing, likes to tan early—and often. Her favorite salon charges $6 a session or $40 for a month of unlimited use. "When I get my paycheck, I'll buy a month, and I'll go every day or every other day," she says. "I try to get in there as much as possible to get my money's worth."

Kennedy is one of the estimated 2.3 million teens who pop into a tanning parlor at least once a year, helping make indoor tanning what an industry trade group says is a $5 billion-a-year business. While many go only in the spring to get ready for the prom, more and more are seeking year-round "bronzitude," according to dermatologists, who are alarmed by the risks of so much exposure to ultraviolet (UV) radiation. A survey of nearly 1,300 teenagers in Boston and Minneapolis-St. Paul, Minn., conducted in 2000 by researchers at Harvard and the University of Minnesota, found that 42% of girls had tried indoor tanning.

Easy access to insta-tans, doctors say, may be contributing to a frightening spike in skin-cancer rates among the young. The incidence of melanoma, the most lethal form of skin cancer, has doubled in the U.S. since 1975 among women ages 15 to 29. This year 2,050 of them are expected to be diagnosed with the malignancy. "Skin cancer used to be something old people got," says Dr. James Spencer, a clinical professor of dermatology at New York City's Mount Sinai School of Medicine. "Not a month goes by that I don't see somebody in their 20s now. That was unheard of 10 years ago."

Doctors worry about the long-term consequences of adolescent tanning. The World Health Organization estimated last week that up to 60,000 deaths worldwide are caused each year by excessive UV exposure and urged youths under 18 to steer clear of indoor tanning.

(http://www.time.com/time/archive/preview/0,10987,1220506,00.html)

Question 1

Which of the following statements most closely describes the concerns about tanning?

A. There are not enough available tanning beds.
B. Many young girls are tanning.
C. UV exposure can cause cancer.
D. Tanning is too expensive.

In this example, A and D are not possible answers. While B appears to be true, it is not as much of a "concern" as C is, making C the better answer of the two. This is a good example of the concept on a multiple-choice test of not choosing the first answer you recognize from the passage. Make sure you read all the choices.

Question 2

Which statement represents the main idea of the article?

A. Tanning may be contributing to the rise in skin cancer among young people.
B. Young people are spending too much money on tanning.
C. The tanning industry is very popular.
D. The tanning industry is taking advantage of young people.

In this example, A is clearly the main idea. Statements B, C, and D all might be true, but considering how much of the article was spent on the health concerns of tanning, A is by far the best choice.

Question 3

How do researchers know how popular tanning is with teens?

A. They observed the changes in pigment of a student body of a high school class.
B. They surveyed students in Boston and Minnesota.
C. They surveyed tanning salon owners.
D. They conducted phone interviews of teenage households.

This is one of those detail questions that you are guaranteed to get correct if you take your time and walk through it. The only possible correct answer—that is, the only answer that is actually mentioned in the article—is B.

Question 4

According to the information in the passage, doctors feel that

A. tanning should be made illegal.
B. teenagers should not be allowed to tan without parental permission.
C. the long-term consequences of tanning may be deadly.
D. tanning for adults is not dangerous.

In this example, you are given several statements that might be true. But, remember, for this standard, you will mostly be dealing with facts from the passage rather than information that you know on your own. Answers A and B are too extreme to be correct. D does not seem logical, and it wasn't discussed in the passage. Therefore, C is the best answer.

Question 5

How does the story of Kylie-Ayn Kennedy affect the article?

A. It proves that all teenagers tan.
B. It shows how popular tanning is in Pennsylvania.
C. It shows that teens are willing to spend their own money tanning and how important it is to them.
D. It shows how much money the tanning industry is making.

This is one of the more challenging ways to ask a detail question. Although the answer is not in the passage word-for-word, you can still use logic and common sense to answer it correctly. You must continue to keep in mind that unless the answer is in the passage, it can't be correct. Statement A is not true, because not all teenagers tan. Even if they did, the story of one girl wouldn't show that. The same is true for B, because this is still only one girl in Pennsylvania. If you look at the reference to her paycheck and how often she tans, C is the best answer. D is not mentioned until later and is not shown with the example of one teenager.

Question 6

The writer's purpose in this article is most likely to

A. shut down the tanning industry.
B. attempt to explain the rise in skin cancer among young people.
C. criticize teens for not taking better care of their health.
D. call for further research into skin cancer prevention.

When asked about an author's purpose, you can first look at the verbs which follow right after the letter choices. You have "shut down," "attempt to explain," "criticize," and "call for." Options A, C, and D use very active verbs, whereas B is passive and informational. When thinking of this passage with its scientific data and statistics, C appears to be the best answer. A is too extreme, and there's no evidence in the passage to support C and D as answers. Now you may think we need to do more research into cancer prevention, and you may feel that this article was picking on teens because of how it was written, but you would be incorrect to assume that that was actually the author's purpose. So B would be the correct answer choice here.

Now that you've seen the different ways that this standard might show up on the OGT, let's try some real practice items.

Use the passage below to answer the following questions:

> While you may not be thinking about it in the haze of this summer's heat, back-to-school season is just around the corner. As parents prepare to reclaim their homes, kids are ready to get their new school clothes and gadgets. However, school essentials are no longer limited to new jeans and a binder. These days, kids' school bags are as important and as identifiable as they are.
>
> In the age of shrinking school budgets, a good backpack choice is important—as backpacks have basically become portable lockers. With the upcoming Backpack Awareness Day on Sept. 20, we have a few ideas as to how parents can choose the right bag for their child.
>
> Increased textbook size and workloads may have students feeling mentally overworked, but the reality is that they're also physically overworked. The American Occupational Therapy Association, sponsors of Backpack Awareness Day, recommend an appropriate weight for backpacks at 15 percent or less of a child's weight—not to ever exceed 25 pounds for children. For teens, the weight should not exceed 15 to 20 percent of their body weight.
>
> Doctor Sarah Gibson of the Queen Anne Chiropractic Center in Seattle notes that "we often get caught up in thinking that 'bigger is better.' In this case it truly is not, as the bigger the backpack is the greater the chances are that things will accumulate in it."
>
> In recent years, companies have gone to great lengths to build better backpacks for back health. Dr. Gibson contends that parents should "be concerned about buying an ergonomic backpack, as pain and injuries are becoming more common in children as of late. It has been shown that greater than 50 percent of youths have at least one episode of low back pain by the end of their teenage years."
>
> Independent research agrees. Studies done by the Consumer Product Safety Commission illustrate that backpack-related injuries among school children have increased by 300 percent since 1996. Other studies have shown that 6 out of 10 students experience chronic back pain related to heavy backpacks.
>
> (http://www.msnbc.msn.com/id/14048836/)

Question 1

The main idea of this passage is that

A. students should not carry backpacks.
B. backpacks can be source of pain.
C. backpacks should be carefully chosen.
D. students don't enjoy using backpacks.

Keeping the concept of "main idea" in mind, meaning that it must be both true and more than just a detail, choice C is the best answer. B is true, but not worthy of being called the "main idea." A and D are too extreme or not supported in the passage.

Question 2

Which of the following statements most closely describes the reasons that backpacks cause injuries?

A. Students carry too much weight in their backpacks.
B. Students are forced to carry backpacks for long periods of time.
C. Parents ask children to carry backpacks at home.
D. Students use backpacks to show off their strength.

According to the details provided in the passage, the main issue behind backpacks is that they are too heavy for young people's bodies. With this in mind, choice A is clearly the best answer. There is no evidence in the passage to support B, C, or D.

Question 3

What is the appropriate ratio of body-to-backpack weight for students?

A. It doesn't matter.
B. The backpack should weigh no more than half the student's weight.
C. The backpack should not exceed 15–20 percent of the student's body weight.
D. The backpack should not exceed 5 percent of the student's body weight.

This question might look scary until you remember that the answer is right there in the passage for you to find when you need it. Looking back over the passage, you'll note that choice C is included word-for-word. On some of the detail questions, it will be just that simple and straightforward. Always look back and locate the correct answer, though, to be certain.

Question 4

"Increased textbook size and workloads may have students feeling mentally overworked, but the reality is that they're also physically overworked."

This sentence from the passage can be paraphrased as:

A. Students work too hard.
B. Students carry too many textbooks.
C. Students' minds and bodies are overworked these days.
D. Students should not carry such large textbooks.

Hopefully you remembered that this question was asking you to restate the sentence in different words without changing the idea. This can be tough, especially if you are given four statements that sound true. Remember that they must restate the given sentence completely, and the only choice that accomplishes that is C.

Consider the following poem to answer sample questions 5 and 6:

Introduction to Poetry

1   I ask them to take a poem
     and hold it up to the light
     like a color slide

2   or press an ear against its hive.

3   I say drop a mouse into a poem
     and watch him probe his way out,

4   or walk inside the poem's room
     and feel the walls for a light switch.

5   I want them to waterski
     across the surface of a poem
     waving at the author's name on the shore.

6   But all they want to do
     is tie the poem to a chair with rope
     and torture a confession out of it.

7   They begin beating it with a hose
     to find out what it really means.

from *The Apple that Astonished Paris* by Billy Collins, 1996
University of Arkansas Press, Fayetteville, Ark.

Question 5

In stanza 7, what major point is the poet making?

A. People are too violent.
B. Poems can inspire readers to action.
C. Readers try too hard to find the meanings of a poem.
D. People should think before they act.

Since this is the last stanza, you will already have picked up on the fact that the poet is describing how readers interact with a poem and how they attempt to discover its meaning. That makes choice C the best answer. Stanza 7 includes the exaggerated metaphor of striking a poem to "torture a confession" out of it, all of which fits in with the rest of the poem.

Question 6

The poet's purpose in the poem is most likely to

A. criticize poets for being too complicated.
B. encourage readers to think and explore when reading a poem.
C. discuss how to teach poetry.
D. amuse the reader with humorous images.

Finding the purpose behind a poem can be challenging. Remember that people write poetry for the same reasons that they write fiction or nonfiction. Look again at the verbs that follow the choices. We have "criticize," "encourage," "discuss," and "amuse." The poem is critical, but not of poets, so A is not the best choice. The speaker seems to be doing more than discussing the teaching of poetry, so C is not the best answer. The poem does have some amusing images in its figurative language, but there seems to be more going on here than an attempt to make the reader laugh. That makes B a better answer than D. If anything, the speaker is critical of the readers of poetry, in that they feel like their job is to do whatever they have to in order to "figure out" a poem.

Chapter 3 Wrap-Up

So there's another standard down! This one was called Reading Process. Here are the key points to remember from this chapter:

- You should feel confident about this standard and the related test questions. Read carefully, use logic and common sense, and the answers will be right there in the passage for you.

- You think about these concepts every time you read, whether it's in English class or reading for pleasure. These skills are going to come naturally to you.

- Like the previous section, don't be tempted to choose the first "possibly correct" answer. Sometimes you have two possible answers, and you must choose the better of the two. It's worth your time to read everything and eliminate all answers until all that remains is the correct one.

- Don't be intimidated by the use of a poem. Follow the same advice on these: take your time and think through the answers.

    It's time to move on to Reading Applications: Informational, Technical, and Persuasive Text.

Reading Applications: Informational, Technical, and Persuasive Text

THE STANDARD

1. Identify and understand organizational patterns (e.g., cause-effect, problem-solution) and techniques, including repetition of ideas, syntax and word choice, that authors use to accomplish their purpose and reach their intended audience.
2. Critique the treatment, scope and organization of ideas from multiple sources on the same topic.
3. Evaluate the effectiveness of information found in maps, charts, tables, graphs, diagrams, cutaways and overlays.
4. Assess the adequacy, accuracy and appropriateness of an author's details, identifying persuasive techniques (e.g., bandwagon, testimonial, transfer, glittering generalities, emotional word repetition, bait and switch) and examples of propaganda, bias and stereotyping.
5. Analyze an author's implicit and explicit argument, perspective or viewpoint in text.
6. Analyze the author's development of key points to support argument or point of view. Identify appeals to authority, reason, and emotion.
7. Analyze the effectiveness of the features (e.g., format, sequence, headers) used in various consumer documents (e.g., warranties, product information, instructional materials), functional or workplace documents (e.g., job-related materials, memoranda, instructions) and public documents (e.g., speeches or newspaper editorials).
8. Describe the features of rhetorical devices used in common types of public documents, including newspaper editorials and speeches.

The Reading OGT will derive 14–19 points from this standard. The questions will be multiple choice, short answer, and extended response.

You can tell as you look over the standard that it is geared toward nonfiction. Also, this standard covers such skills as analyzing, identifying, evaluating, and describing.

This being the case, if you like math and science, this will be right up your alley. Don't worry if you are not an analytical person, though. You will see in the examples that there are techniques that will help you be successful no matter what type of reading you are asked to do.

The Standard in Action

When you are asked questions that test this standard, it is likely that you will be asked what an author is suggesting or why an author includes certain information in a passage. You may also be asked what techniques an author uses to be viewed as credible or worth believing. One unique question from this standard might ask you to describe something to help a reader better understand the ideas in the passage. It is likely that you will also be asked to think about the kinds of evidence that the author is providing. This is very similar to what you are asked to do in several other parts of the test—find information in the passage. Sometimes the question will pull out a quote from the passage and ask you which one supports a certain idea. Finally, you may be asked to explain why the title is appropriate, which should tell you that there is something about the title that connects to what the author is trying to show or prove. Remember, this is nonfiction.

What the Standard Looks Like on the Actual OGT

Following the passage below, you will be asked questions that are phrased in the following manners:

- The author includes this in the passage in order to show . . .

- The author suggests that . . .

- Which technique does the author use to have readers view the information presented in the article as credible?

- Describe a picture or other graphic that would help a reader more clearly understand or be more interested in the ideas given in the passage.

- How does the author surprise the reader?

- What was the evidence presented?

- What evidence does the author present?

- Which quotation supports the author's view that . . .

- According to the information given in the passage . . .

- Explain how the title of the article is an especially appropriate one.

Consider the following article when answering the practice questions for Informational, technical, and persuasive text:

> LONDON—British actor Daniel Radcliffe has signed up for the final two films in the seven-part Harry Potter series, his spokeswoman said on Friday.
>
> The 17-year-old, who has just won rave reviews for his performance in Peter Shaffer's controversial play "Equus," will start filming the sixth movie, "Harry Potter and the Half-Blood Prince" by J.K. Rowling, in September, she added.

Radcliffe shot to fame in 2001 when he appeared as the boy wizard in the first Harry Potter film.

The hit franchise, which continues with the fifth installment called "Harry Potter and the Order of the Phoenix" later this year, has amassed around $3.5 billion globally at the box office and turned the teenager into a multi-millionaire.

Rowling recently announced that the seventh and final book in the series, called "Harry Potter and the Deathly Hallows" will be published on July 21, but it is not clear when the film version will be made.

The first six books have sold in excess of 325 million copies worldwide.

(http://www.msnbc.msn.com/id/17421349/)

Question 1

What evidence does the author present to show the success of the Harry Potter franchise?

A. testimonials
B. charts and graphs
C. sales amounts and figures
D. author opinion

In this case, you will note that the piece mentions both monetary figures as well as copies sold, so C is the best answer.

Question 2

What technique does the writer use to have the readers view the information in the article as credible?

A. The article quotes the author.
B. The writer discusses different titles of plays and movies.
C. The article is short.
D. The writer uses many dates.

Although the article does quote the author, the fact that the writer knows about several movies and plays seems to indicate that he is knowledgeable about the industry, making B the best answer.

Read the next article for the remaining sample questions in this chapter.

Verizon Begins Cell Phone TV Service

Verizon Wireless on Thursday launched a broadcast TV service for cell phones in about 20 Midwestern and Western markets, charging $15 to $25 a month for the initial lineup from eight leading networks.

While Verizon had already said it planned to introduce the service this month, the launch provided this country's first detailed glimpse of the features and pricing for a long-awaited next wave in cellular technology.

Notably, the launch came one day after a demonstration in New York of a planned rival broadcast service called Modeo, as well as an announcement by MobiTV, a forerunner to these new offerings, that it has reached 2 million users.

V Cast Mobile TV, delivered over a separate wireless network operated by Qualcomm Inc., requires a new handset capable of receiving the broadcast signal in addition to the regular cellular signal for phone calls and mobile Internet access.

The eight 24-hour channels are CBS Mobile, Comedy Central, ESPN, Fox Mobile, MTV, NBC 2Go, NBC News 2Go and Nickelodeon. While most of the programming will be identical to that shown by those networks on regular TV, only some shows will be broadcast at the same time.

For example: the MTV broadcast will be identical around the clock; CBS Mobile will show some daytime soap operas at different hours, but feature simultaneous showings of the *CBS Evening News, Survivor* and the *Late Show With David Letterman*; on Comedy Central, *The Daily Show* and the *The Colbert Report* will be shown at their normal hour, but *South Park, Reno 911* and *Chappelle's Show* will be time-shifted.

Verizon Wireless, owned jointly by Verizon Communications Inc. and Vodafone Group PLC, is offering the broadcast TV lineup either as a stand-alone product for $15 a month, or bundled for $25 a month with the company's mobile Web access and the wide-ranging library of V Cast video clip downloads. The first dual-mode handset from Samsung Electronics Co. costs $200 without signing a new Verizon service contract, or $50 less with a new commitment. Verizon Wireless expects to introduce a second handset made by LG Electronics Co. in the coming weeks.

The biggest markets for the initial launch of V Cast Mobile TV signal are Chicago, Dallas-Fort Worth, Denver, Kansas City, Las Vegas, Minneapolis-St. Paul, New Orleans, St. Louis, Salt Lake City and Seattle.

The service is also available in Portland, Ore., Tuscon, Ariz., Omaha and Lincoln in Nebraska, the Albuquerque-Santa Fe region of New Mexico; Palm Springs, Calif., Colorado Springs, Colo., Jacksonville, Fla., Wichita, Kan., the Norfolk-Richmond region of Virginia, and Spokane, Wash.

In addition to Verizon, Qualcomm has signed on AT&T Inc.'s Cingular Wireless to offer the MediaFlo TV service, though that launch isn't expected until late this year.

Modeo, which is being developed by cellular tower operator Crown Castle International Corp., is running a trial of its service in the New York City area with six TV channels, but has yet to announce any wireless providers to carry its service.

At the presentation Wednesday night, Modeo stressed that the potential market for mobile TV included laptops and other portable devices, and that the venture was forging ahead regardless of MediaFlo's win with the two biggest U.S. carriers.

Question 3

Describe a picture or other graphic that would help a reader more clearly understand or be more interested in the ideas given in the passage.

This would be given to you as an extended-response question, and you would have to provide evidence to support your choice. Think about what was discussed in the passage, though. Several good options are there. For example, there were many cities mentioned, so a map might help the reader visually understand where the services were being offered. Also, there were references to amounts of money being made, and oftentimes it's easier to understand those types of comparisons when seen on a bar graph or pie chart. We will discuss more about short-answer and extended-response questions in Chapter 6.

Question 4

The author mentions the launch of the new Verizon service "came one day after a demonstration in New York of a planned rival broadcast service called Modeo, as well as an announcement by MobiTV, a forerunner to these new offerings, that it has reached 2 million users" in order to

A. show that Verizon works fast.
B. prove that Verizon has excellent service.
C. suggest that Verizon reacted to competition.
D. suggest that the competition is better than Verizon.

In this example, several of the statements are potentially true, but if you looked back in the article (which you should always do), you will see that based on when this detail was mentioned within the article, it's clear that C is the best answer. There was a definite connection between Verizon's launch and what the competition was doing.

Question 5

Which quotation supports the author's view that the new cell phone TV service is not the same as regular television?

A. Although most of the programming will be identical to that shown by those networks on regular TV, only some shows will be broadcast at the same time.
B. V Cast Mobile TV, delivered over a separate wireless network operated by Qualcomm Inc., requires a new handset capable of receiving the broadcast signal in addition to the regular cellular signal for phone calls and mobile Internet access.
C. Though Verizon had already said it planned to introduce the service this month, the launch provided this country's first detailed glimpse of the features and pricing for a long-awaited next wave in cellular technology.
D. In addition to Verizon, Qualcomm, Inc. has signed on AT&T Inc.'s Cingular Wireless to offer the MediaFlo TV service, though that launch isn't expected until late this year.

I'm sure you noticed right away that when you're asked a question like this, you have to do more reading. Not only do you have to read the question, but you also have to read the quotations even if they are lengthy. But, don't let that bother you. Remember, you have already read the article once. First, follow your routine in terms of test-taking strategies. Are there any answers that are not related closely enough to the question? Option D looks like it is not a valid choice. While B and C do discuss differences, A is the only one that specifically discusses differences in the actual service, making it the correct answer.

Chapter 4 Wrap-Up

Another standard down! This one was called Reading Applications: Informational, Technical, and Persuasive Text. Here are the key points to remember from this chapter:

• This standard and related test questions are likely to be about nonfiction, which you may find interesting.

• You have been answering questions like this for years in school and on other tests you've taken—you've done this a lot!

• Your test-taking skills will still help you: Read the question carefully, go back and look at the articles to make sure you understand the question, eliminate any obviously wrong answers, and don't make assumptions about the answers that aren't supported in the passages.

It's time to move on to Reading Applications: Literary Text.

Reading Applications: Literary Text

THE STANDARD

1. Compare and contrast an author's use of direct and indirect characterization, and ways in which characters reveal traits about themselves, including dialect, dramatic monologues and soliloquies.
2. Analyze the features of setting and their importance in a literary text.
3. Identify ways in which authors use conflicts, parallel plots and subplots in literary texts.
4. Distinguish how conflicts, parallel plots and subplots affect the pacing of action in a literary text.
5. Evaluate the point of view used in a literary text.
6. Interpret universal themes across different works by the same author and different authors.
7. Analyze how an author's choice of genre affects the expression of a theme or topic.
8. Explain how literary techniques including foreshadowing and flashback are used to shape plot in a literary text.
9. Recognize how types of irony, including verbal, situational and dramatic, are used in literary texts.
10. Analyze author's use of mood and tone through word choice, figurative language and syntax.
11. Explain how authors use symbols to create broader meanings.
12. Describe the effect of sound devices, including alliteration, assonance, consonance and onomatopoeia, used in literary texts.
13. Explain ways in which an author develops a point of view and style (e.g., figurative language, sentence structure and tone), and cite specific examples from the text.

The Reading OGT will derive 10–16 points from this standard. The questions will be multiple choice, short answer, and extended response.

That's quite a list, isn't it? But these are the skills that all great English classes are made of! It is likely that you have already been doing most of these things in your English classes for years—you've even been practicing the skills in other classes, too, but probably not using fiction and poetry. Beyond the OGT, these are also skills that will help you on the ACT, SAT, in any other high school English class, and even into college and beyond.

The Standard in Action

You may be asked questions like the following in this section:

- Which statement below describes the tone in the final paragraph of the passage?

- Which of the statements below best describes a theme of the passage?

- Explain how a concept is developed in the story (extended response).

- Which of the excerpts illustrates the narrator's sense of . . .

- What was the author's purpose in telling. . .

- Explain how the author emphasizes . . . (short answer)

- Which statement best represents the theme of the poem?

- Which statement best represents the writer's intended meaning?

Some of these concepts are very much like what you have already been asked to do in different sections of the test.

You should also be prepared to do some analytical thinking about two different stories or poems. You'll notice in the standards that you may be asked to compare "universal themes" in two different works. This simply means that it is a common and obvious theme that you should easily be able to determine after reading the poems or stories. A universal theme, for example, might be, "As humans, we should be tolerant of each other's differences." You can see how it would be possible for two poems to send this same message but in a different way. Don't let this type of question bother you. Again, it's what you already do in English class and other classes all the time.

Read the following short story and try the sample questions:

"The Princess and the Tin Box"
by James Thurber

Once upon a time, in a far country, there lived a King whose daughter was the prettiest princess in the world. Her eyes were like the cornflower, her hair was sweeter than the hyacinth, and her throat made the swan look dusty.

From the time she was a year old, the Princess had been showered with presents. Her nursery looked like Cartier's window. Her toys were all made of gold or platinum or diamonds or emeralds. She was not permitted to have wooden blocks or china dolls or rubber dogs or linen books, because such materials were considered cheap for the daughter of a king.

When she was seven, she was allowed to attend the wedding of her brother and throw real pearls at the bride instead of rice. Only the nightingale, with his lyre of gold, was permitted to sing for the Princess. The common blackbird, with his boxwood flute, was kept out of the palace grounds. She walked in silver-and-samite slippers to a sapphire-and-topaz bathroom and slept in an ivory bed inlaid with rubies.

On the day the Princess was eighteen, the King sent a royal ambassador to the courts of five neighboring kingdoms to announce that he would give his daughter's hand in marriage to the prince who brought her the gift she liked the most.

The first prince to arrive at the palace rode a swift white stallion and laid at the feet of the Princess an enormous apple made of solid gold which he had taken from a dragon who had guarded it for a thousand years. It was placed on a long ebony table set up to hold the gifts of the Princess' suitors. The second prince, who came on a gray charger, brought her a nightingale made of a thousand diamonds, and it was placed beside the golden apple. The third prince, riding on a black horse, carried a great jewel box made of platinum and sapphires, and it was placed next to the diamond nightingale. The fourth prince, astride a fiery yellow horse, gave the Princess a gigantic heart made of rubies and pierced by an emerald arrow. It was placed next to the platinum-and-sapphire jewel box.

Now the fifth prince was the strongest and handsomest of all the five suitors, but he was the son of a poor king whose realm had been overrun by mice and locusts and wizards and mining engineers so that there was nothing much of value left in it. He came plodding up to the palace of the Princess on a plow horse, and he brought her a small tin box filled with mica and feldspar and hornblende (types of ordinary rocks) which he had picked up on the way.

The other princes roared with disdainful laughter when they saw the tawdry gift the fifth prince had brought to the Princess. But she examined it with great interest and squealed with delight, for all her life she had been glutted with precious stones and priceless metals, but she had never seen tin before or mica or feldspar or hornblende. The tin box was placed next to the ruby heart pierced with an emerald arrow.

"Now," the King said to his daughter, "you must select the gift you like best and marry the prince that brought it."

The Princess smiled and walked up to the table and picked up the present she liked the most. It was the platinum-and-sapphire jewel box, the gift of the third prince.

"The way I figure it," she said, "is this. It is a very large and expensive box, and when I am married, I will meet many admirers who will give me precious gems with which to fill it to the top. Therefore, it is the most valuable of all the gifts my suitors have brought me, and I like it the best."

The Princess married the third prince that very day in the midst of great merriment and high revelry. More than a hundred thousand pearls were thrown at her and she loved it.

Moral: *All those who thought that the Princess was going to select the tin box filled with worthless stones instead of one of the other gifts will kindly stay after class and write one hundred times on the blackboard, "I would rather have a hunk of aluminum silicate than a diamond necklace."*

Question 1

Which of the following statements best represents the theme of the story?

A. Wealth is not important.
B. Sometimes people can be greedy.
C. Human nature doesn't often change.
D. Fairy tales do come true.

Since the story is meant to be humorous or sarcastic, the writer has the Princess choose the large and expensive gift instead of the gift from the poor and handsome prince. This being the case, A and D are poor choices. Because her choice of gifts makes the Princess seem greedy, the better answer between B and C is B, even though the moral that follows supports that Thurber is discussing human nature, too.

Question 2

Which of the excerpts illustrates the sense of pride of the King?

A. She was not permitted to have wooden blocks or china dolls or rubber dogs or linen books, because such materials were considered cheap for the daughter of a king.
B. The fourth prince, astride a fiery yellow horse, gave the Princess a gigantic heart made of rubies and pierced by an emerald arrow.
C. More than a hundred thousand pearls were thrown at her and she loved it.
D. On the day the Princess was eighteen, the King sent a royal ambassador to the courts of five neighboring kingdoms to announce that he would give his daughter's hand in marriage to the prince who brought her the gift she liked the most.

In this sample, B and C are not closely related to the question about the King's pride. D sounds as if the King has wealth and high hopes for his daughter. But A is the one that best shows the king's pride.

Question 3

Which best describes the tone of the last paragraph, the moral?

A. indifferent
B. angry
C. hopeful
D. sarcastic

The moral is not mean or angry, so B is out. Also, it does not seem very positive, so we can eliminate C. Between A and D, if you consider the entire story and how he tells it, he is being sarcastic. He is teasing the readers about whether they themselves would actually choose handsome and poor over expensive.

Question 4

Explain how the concept of humor is used in the story. Use three details or examples from the story to support your answer.

This would be a 4-pt. extended-response question, but we can at least practice how to answer it. First, fill in a sentence below that answers the first part of the question—how is humor used?

In the passage, humor is used to

_____

_____

_____

Read over what you wrote. Hopefully you went beyond the definition of "humor," which is to make someone laugh or amuse. Remember, you're being asked to analyze here. Perhaps you mentioned that the humor helps the reader see how funny people's reactions can be sometimes. Or maybe you mentioned that humor makes the point about human nature stronger. You will earn 1 of the 4 points for making a reasonable attempt to say how the author uses humor.

Now for the remaining three points, look back at what you wrote and list three examples of humor from the piece. You can quote the story if that's the best way for you to give your three examples. If you don't quote, be very specific.

example 1: _____

_____

example 2: _____

_____

example 3: _____

_____

Remember, to score all the points, your examples should support what you said about how the author used humor not just any example of humor.

Some use of humor in the story includes the poetic language, exaggeration, what the Princess says at the end, how the author describes the Princess as loving the pearls that were thrown at her, and suggesting that the readers should have to write on the blackboard if they expected an unrealistic ending.

One of the keys to a question like this is to be sure to put all four parts in: answer the question, and give three examples. It is common that students who miss points on this question simply do not do all four parts.

Question 5

What was the author's purpose in describing the gifts brought to the princess in such great detail?

A. to hold the readers' interest
B. to show the wealth and character of the different princes
C. to show the wealth of the king
D. to emphasize the humor in the story

In this case, since the description is attached to the arrival of each new prince and it does much to show how rich (or poor) each prince is, B is the best answer. Choice A might be true, but it's unlikely that it is why the author includes the detail. C does not make sense, and D is not likely to be true because the description was very factual.

Now let's try some questions about poetry. If you like poetry, you'll find these easy. If you don't like poetry, you will still be able to answer the questions correctly if you follow the steps that you've been learning here.

Read the poem below and try the questions that follow.

"Mother to Son"
by Langston Hughes

Well, son, I'll tell you:
Life for me ain't been no crystal stair.
It's had tacks in it,
Line And splinters,
(5) And boards torn up,
And places with no carpet on the floor—
Bare.
But all the time
I'se been a-climbin' on,
(10) And reachin' landin's,
And turnin' corners,
And sometimes goin' in the dark
Where there ain't been no light.
So, boy, don't you turn back.
(15) Don't you set down on the steps.
'Cause you finds it's kinder hard.
Don't you fall now—
For I'se still goin', honey,
I'se still climbin',
(20) And life for me ain't been no crystal stair.

Question 6

Based on the poem, what sentence gives the best interpretation of "life for me ain't been no crystal stair"?

A. Life for me is beautiful.
B. Life for me is full of wealth.
C. Life for me has been difficult.
D. Life for me has been to please you.

Since the speaker says that life "ain't" been positive, then you know to look for a choice that's negative. If you think about how the speaker describes her stair as having tacks and splinters, it makes C jump right out.

Question 7

Which of the following best represents the theme of the poem?

A. Life is not worth living.
B. Never give up because I haven't.
C. We never get what we want in life.
D. People who are given things in life are successful.

If you think about the lines in the poem where the speaker says, "So, boy, don't you turn back / Don't you set down on the steps / 'Cause you finds it's kinder hard. / Don't you fall now," it seems to be a voice that's coaching the child or that's trying to inspire the child to keep trying. This makes B the best answer choice.

Question 8

Which of the following best represents the meaning of a "crystal stair"?

A. easy path
B. fancy life
C. fragile life
D. easy way of getting help

This one is tougher, since "crystal stair" is a metaphor. It gives you an image of climbing, and crystal is valuable. If you put those together, and think about how stairs are a way that we climb higher, option A becomes the best choice. It would have helped you again to remember how the speaker describes what her stair was like, as she does in lines 1–7. Put simply, she has had a tough time, not one that has been fancy and easy.

Chapter 5 Wrap-Up

See, that wasn't so bad! This one was called Reading Applications: Literary Text. Here are the key points to remember from this chapter:

- This standard and the related test questions are likely to be about fiction and poetry, which many students enjoy and find more interesting than nonfiction.

- You have been answering questions like this for years in school and on other tests you've taken—you've already done this a lot! To be good at it you must take your time and read carefully.

- It will help you to make quick notes in the passages as you read and to use underlining, bracketing, and circling to note parts of the stories or poems that you have thoughts about. It helps keep you active and alert, and it is likely that you will come back to those places to answer the questions.
  It's time to discuss how to earn all the points on the short-answer and extended-response sections of the Reading OGT.

Time Out! Scoring Well on the Short-Answer and Extended-Response Sections of the Reading OGT

A t this point, you've seen all of the standards for the Reading OGT, the types of passages and questions you'll be given, and sample questions and techniques for getting those questions correct. Now it's time to focus in on the two types of questions that are worth the most points: short-answer and extended-response.

On the Reading OGT, the short-answer section will make up 8 points (four at 2 pts. each), and the extended-response section will also make up 8 points (two at 4 pts. each).

The long reading passage you're given on the Reading OGT will be assessed with one extended-response question and up to two short-answer questions. A medium passage is assessed with either one short-answer or one extended-response question. Short passages will not be assessed with extended-response questions. These passages will only have one short-answer question.

Why is all of that important? Is the 3-point line important in basketball? You bet it is! It's important that you understand that these types of questions are just as crucial as that line on the basketball court! Each time you encounter a short-answer or extended-response question, you have either 2 or 4 points on the line. Plus, you aren't just bubbling in an answer; you have to find the correct place in the answer document to complete your response. It increases the odds that you might make a mistake.

We have already discussed how to address questions like this, but now we'll get more specific and make sure you know how to get all of the available points. You may be wondering if your writing is graded in addition to your ideas. That's a good question, considering that this is the Reading OGT. The answer is no. Your actual writing is not part of the scoring of the Reading OGT. But don't think about that. Just write your best. Remember, these are scored by human beings, not computers. Believe that neatness and quality writing can make a difference, even if only a little bit.

SHORT-ANSWER RESPONSES

When you are faced with one of these, keep in mind that there are specific items that the scorers are looking for. Take a question like this:

> Explain what the author means AND give a detail or example from the passage to support your idea.

First you must answer the question by writing what you believe the author means (by a line that you're given). That is worth one point of the two. Then you write down a detail or a quote from the story. Be careful, though. It must be from the story, which seems obvious. It also must support what you wrote in response to the first part of the question. They have to connect!

Here's how it would be scored officially:

Score	Description
2 pts.	The response provides a reasonable explanation for what the author means by the given expression and gives an appropriate detail or example from the passage in support.
1 pt.	The response provides a reasonable explanation for what the author means by the given expression but does not give an appropriate detail or example from the passage in support.
0 pts.	The response does not provide sufficient evidence of understanding the task.

I hope you notice some of the key words in the scoring descriptions. They say "reasonable" explanation. The scorers will have a list of possible responses, but they are trained to work with what you give them and to be supportive in considering if it is "reasonable." Also, you need an "appropriate" detail in support of the passage. That means, as I said earlier, that it must match what you wrote as the reasonable explanation.

It all sounds pretty easy, right? But sometimes students don't understand the passages as well as they want to and that affects their answers. Also, sometimes students try to rush and leave out part of the answer. Leaving out one point might not seem like much, but you wouldn't tell an opponent in basketball that you want your made baskets to count for only one point, would you? Get all the points that you can every time.

EXTENDED-RESPONSE ANSWERS

These might seem a little tougher than short-answer responses. That makes sense. After all, you have twice as many parts to include in your answer. But much like short-answer responses, if you take your time and work carefully, you will get all four points!

Take a look at this sample question:

> Explain how the title of the article is an especially appropriate one. Support your explanation by giving three examples or details from the passage.

If you think it through, you come up with a very clear job. Give four pieces of information: how the title is appropriate, and three reasons to support that. If it helps you to number each response, go ahead. It isn't part of the scoring, and it might help you to check your work.

Here's how it would be scored officially:

Score	Description
4 pts.	The response provides a plausible explanation that is supported by three appropriate examples or details from the story.
3 pts.	The response provides a plausible explanation that is supported by two appropriate examples or details from the story.
2 pts.	The response provides a plausible explanation that is supported by one appropriate example or detail from the story.
1 pt.	The response provides a plausible explanation, but it is not supported with an appropriate example or detail from the story.
0 pts.	The response does not provide sufficient evidence of understanding the task.

Yes, it's a bit more complicated than the short-answer response, but you can still get all of the points. Think about it. It's really just an extension of the short-answer response. On those, you could have provided more examples, but they only ask for one. Also, consider some of the words in the extended-response scoring language. Guess what "plausible" means? That's right—it means about the same as "reasonable." And they have emphasized that your example must be "appropriate," meaning it must "fit" what you write in the first part that answers their question, about the title in this case.

Let's look at a sample short-answer question, sample responses, and how they would score:

Remember in Chapter 4 when we discussed a question like "Describe a picture or other graphic that would help a reader more clearly understand or be more interested in the ideas given in the passage"? Let's try something like that with Sample question 3 in that chapter. It was the article about TV service on cell phones. Here is the official question:

> Describe a picture or other graphic that would help a reader more clearly understand or be more interested in the ideas given in the passage. Give two specific examples from the passage that support your choice of a picture or other graphic.

First, you must answer the question by describing a graphic. Then, you must provide two examples that "fit" your choice of picture or graphic. Remember to keep track and make sure you provide all of the parts.

SAMPLE RESPONSE

A graphic that could be used to help the reader more clearly understand or be more interested in the ideas given in the passage is a map. The passage mentions several cities such as Denver and Kansas City. A map would help the reader see how far across the country the service could reach. The article also mentions the largest markets for the "initial launch" of the service, and a map would help a reader see if he would be able to get the new service soon.

This would score 2/2 points. It describes a graphic (map) and provides two specific examples from the passage that clearly support the usefulness of the graphic (showing cities for reach of service and showing cities where initial service will begin).

Notice how this response incorporates the question into the answer, which helps keep the writer focused and allows her to check to make sure she is actually answering the question. Also, she quotes a part of the article in the second part of the answer, which makes it more specific. There are no errors in the writing, which makes it look neat and that can only help.

Let's look at a sample from en extended-response question.

Review the story "The Princess and the Tin Box" from Chapter 5. Let's see how an extended-response answer would look for this question:

> Explain how the concept of irony is used in the story. Use three details or examples from the story to support your answer.

There are three types of irony: situational, where something unexpected happens; dramatic, where the reader knows more than the characters; and verbal, which is where words are used for more than the literal or obvious, such as exaggeration or sarcasm.

As with the short-answer responses, you must be clear about what you are being asked and you must respond to all the parts.

SAMPLE RESPONSE

The writer uses both situational and verbal irony to make the story more humorous. The situational irony is funny because the reader expects the Princess to choose the handsome but poor prince and live happily ever after. Instead, she chooses the prince who has the most wealth. Also, the verbal irony is funny in the exaggeration of the gifts being brought by each prince. Later, it says "more than a hundred thousand pearls were thrown at her" on her wedding day. Finally, in the "moral" section, the writer sarcastically tells the reader to write on the blackboard if we would have chosen the box of rocks vs. the wealth.

This would score a 4/4 because it provides a plausible explanation that is supported by three appropriate details or examples from the passage. The explanation is that irony is used to make the story more humorous.

Example 1: the Princess chooses something the reader didn't expect.

Example 2: the exaggeration of the gifts and the pearls being thrown.

Example 3: the sarcasm in the end about writing on the blackboard if we say we would want a box of rocks.

Note that more examples don't hurt you; you must have the required three. Also note that transitions are used to help both the writer and the scorer to see the different parts of the response.

Chapter 6 Wrap-Up

Here's a recap of the most important ways to score all possible points on the short-answer and extended-response questions on the Reading OGT.

- The obvious: Answer the question! Give exactly what you are asked for and exactly how many pieces of support are requested.

- Make sure your support is "appropriate" and fits what you give as your main reason.

- Be organized, numbering your responses if you want. If you can't label the different parts of the question in your response, it might mean that you missed something.

- Even though your actual writing is not scored, do your best work. Do what you can to increase your odds of scoring higher. Sometimes perception can be reality.

- Remember that an extended-response answer is just that: an extension of the short-answer response. Getting full points on both is something you *can* do!

PART 2

THE WRITING OGT

An Overview—What's on the Writing OGT?

CHAPTER 7

It's time now to talk about how to pass and score well on the Ohio Graduation Test in Writing. Usually, the Reading test that we just reviewed and practiced is administered on the Monday of OGT week, and the Writing test is administered on Wednesday. This one day break in between may allow you that extra time to do any final brushing up before you take the Writing test after you've seen how the room will be set up and you have a sense of how all of the testing procedures will work.

The three Writing Content Standards that are tested on the OGT Writing test are Writing Processes, Writing Applications, and Writing Conventions. There will be a chapter for each of these, but here's a quick overview:

WRITING PROCESSES

This category covers quite a bit of skills that you must have in order to be an effective writer. As is the case for much of the material on the OGT, you have been working on developing these skills for many years. That should give you confidence. In this section, you will be asked to demonstrate such concepts as developing a thesis statement, planning for an audience, paragraph structure and use of topic sentences, using precise language, revising for clarity, and proofreading and evaluating your own writing. This sounds like a lot, but if you think about it, it's what you do any time you complete a large writing assignment for English or any other class. Put simply, it's the process of creating good writing.

WRITING APPLICATIONS

This category covers the major types of writing that you might be asked to complete. There are typically three different types to master in this section.

A narrative is a story, and if asked to write a narrative, you'd need to make sure it had all the parts of any good story. We'll get into more detail on that later.

You might be asked to write a letter, such as a business letter or a letter to the editor. This type of writing requires that you write in a style appropriate to the given audience, such as a principal of a school or the mayor of your city.

You might be asked to write a persuasive composition in which you are asked to convince the reader to agree with your opinion. This can be anything from changing a state law to convincing your parents to allow you to go to a basketball camp out of state. The good news is that we use persuasive techniques every day of our lives, so this will not be too challenging for you.

WRITING CONVENTIONS

This category is made up of the nuts and bolts of writing: mechanics, usage, grammar, and spelling (known as MUGS). It also covers the use of clauses, phrases, modifiers (adjectives and adverbs), verb tenses, and other finer points of grammar. Once again, it is likely that you have been learning and practicing how to use these elements effectively in school all along, so brushing up and practicing here will help you to raise your score and get as many points as possible.

THE OGT WRITING TEST

The actual Writing OGT will have ten multiple-choice questions (not bad after surviving 44 on the Reading OGT!). It will also have one short-answer response worth 2 points and two Writing Prompts worth 18 points each. That makes the total number of points available 48. Here's how they arrive at the numbers for the Writing Prompts: There is a 6-point scale for Writing Applications and a 3-point scale for Writing Conventions. That's only 9 points, but each Writing Prompt is scored by two readers and added together, not averaged, doubling the points available to 18.

Here are the two different rubrics or scales used to evaluate Writing Applications (6-point scale) and Writing Conventions (3-point scale).

Writing Applications

HOLISTIC RUBRIC FOR THE OHIO GRADUATION TEST IN WRITING

6   This is a superior piece of writing. The prompt is directly addressed, and the response is effectively adapted to audience and purpose. It is exceptionally developed, containing compelling ideas, examples and details. The response, using a clearly evident organizational plan, actively engages the reader with a unified and coherent sequence and structure of ideas. The response consistently uses a variety of sentence structures, effective word choices and an engaging style.

5   This is an excellent piece of writing. The prompt is directly addressed and the response is clearly adapted to audience and purpose. It is very well-developed, containing strong ideas, examples and details. The response, using a clearly evident organizational plan, engages the reader with a unified and coherent sequence and structure of ideas. The response typically uses a variety of sentence structures, effective word choices and an engaging style.

4   This is an effective piece of writing. While the prompt is addressed and the response adapts to audience and purpose, there are occasional inconsistencies in the response's overall plan. The response is well-developed, containing effective ideas, examples and details. The response, using a good organizational plan, presents the reader with a generally unified and coherent sequence and

structure of ideas. The response often uses a variety of sentence structures, appropriate word choices and an effective style.

3 This is an adequate piece of writing. While the prompt is generally addressed and the response shows an awareness of audience and purpose, there are inconsistencies in the response's overall plan. Although the response contains ideas, examples and details, they are repetitive, unevenly developed and occasionally inappropriate. The response, using an acceptable organizational plan, presents the reader with a generally unified and coherent sequence and structure of ideas. The response occasionally uses a variety of sentence structures, appropriate word choices and an effective style.

2 This is a marginal piece of writing. While an attempt is made to address the prompt, the response shows at best an inconsistent awareness of audience and purpose. When ideas, examples and details are present, they are frequently repetitive, unevenly developed and occasionally inappropriate. The response, using a limited organizational plan, does not present the reader with a generally unified and coherent sequence and structure of ideas. The response is exemplified by noticeable lapses in sentence structure, use of appropriate word choices and a clear, readable style.

1 This is an inadequate piece of writing. There is a weak attempt made to address the prompt. The response shows little or no awareness of audience and purpose. There is little or no development of ideas, or the response is limited to paraphrasing the prompt. There is little or no evidence of organizational structure. The response is exemplified by severe lapses in sentence structure, use of appropriate word choices and a clear, readable style.

0 The following are categories of papers that cannot be scored: off task (complete disregard for the writing task identified by the prompt), completely illegible, in a language other than English, or no response.

CONVENTIONS RUBRIC FOR THE OHIO GRADUATION TEST IN WRITING

3 The written response is free from errors that impair a reader's understanding and comprehension. Few errors, if any, are present in capitalization, punctuation and spelling. The writing displays a consistent understanding of grammatical conventions.

2 Occasional errors may impair a reader's understanding of the written response. Some capitalization, punctuation and spelling errors are present. The writing displays some understanding of grammatical conventions.

1 Errors are frequent and impair a reader's understanding of the written response. Numerous errors in capitalization, punctuation and spelling are present. The writing displays a minimal understanding of grammatical conventions.

0 The following are categories of papers that cannot be scored: completely illegible, in a language other than English, or no response.

OR

The length and complexity of the response is insufficient to demonstrate the writer has control over standard English conventions.

Here are the performance ranges for the Writing OGT for 2006.

	Raw Score	Scaled Score
Advanced	42–48	476–575
Accelerated	33–41.5	430–475
Proficient	24.0–32.5	400–429
— — — — — — — — — — — — —passing line— — — — — — — — — — — — —		
Basic	15.5–23.5	378–399
Limited	0–15	276–377

That's how the five different levels break down for the Writing OGT. It's probably a good idea just to buckle down and plan to do the best you can on every question and let the levels work themselves out. Our focus here is to help you score as many points as you can, and if you follow the strategies outlined in this resource, you will likely find yourself in the Accelerated or Advanced category. Now let's take a closer look at the different sections of the Writing OGT.

Writing Processes

THE STANDARD

1. Generate writing ideas through discussions with others and from printed material, and keep a list of writing ideas.
2. Determine the usefulness of and apply appropriate pre-writing tasks (e.g., background reading, interviews or surveys).
3. Establish and develop a clear thesis statement for informational writing or a clear plan or outline for narrative writing.
4. Determine a purpose and audience and plan strategies (e.g., adapting focus, content structure and point of view) to address purpose and audience.
5. Use organizational strategies (e.g., notes and outlines) to plan writing.
6. Organize writing to create a coherent whole with an effective and engaging introduction, body and conclusion, and a closing sentence that summarizes, extends or elaborates on points or ideas in the writing.
7. Use a variety of sentence structures and lengths (e.g., simple, compound and complex sentences; parallel or repetitive sentence structure).
8. Use paragraph form in writing, including topic sentences that arrange paragraphs in a logical sequence, using effective transitions and closing sentences and maintaining coherence across the whole through the use of parallel structures.
9. Use precise language, action verbs, sensory details, colorful modifiers and style as appropriate to audience and purpose and use techniques to convey a personal style and voice.
10. Use available technology to compose text.
11. Reread and analyze clarity of writing, consistency of point of view and effectiveness of organizational structure.
12. Add and delete information and details to better elaborate on stated central idea and more effectively accomplish purpose.
13. Rearrange words, sentences and paragraphs, and add transitional words and phrases to clarify meaning and maintain consistent style, tone and voice.

Drafting, Revising and Editing

14. Use resources and reference materials (e.g., dictionaries and thesauruses) to select effective and precise vocabulary that maintains consistent style, tone and voice.
15. Proofread writing, edit to improve conventions (e.g., grammar, spelling, punctuation and capitalization), identify and correct fragments and run-ons and eliminate inappropriate slang or informal language.
16. Apply tools (e.g., rubric, checklist and feedback) to judge the quality of writing.

Publishing

17. Prepare for publication (e.g., for display or for sharing with others) writing that follows a manuscript form appropriate for the purpose, which could include such techniques as electronic resources, principles of design (e.g., margins, tabs, spacing and columns) and graphics (e.g., drawings, charts and graphs) to enhance the final product.

It's worth noting again that although there are 17 different parts to the Writing Processes Standard, these are the skills that you have worked on year after year, and these are the skills that make up quality and effective writing. What we will focus on next are the skills that can be evaluated on a test, such as the Writing OGT.

Most of the points for Writing Processes will come in the form of multiple-choice questions. It is also likely that the 2-point short-answer question will test this as well. Of course, the good news about multiple-choice questions on the Writing OGT is that you are only given four choices for your answers, presenting you with a 25 percent chance of choosing the correct answer even if you guess! You'll be way past simply guessing after completing this book, so you should feel good about your odds. The other good part about multiple choice is that you are given the answers to choose from, and you can keep rereading them and using the process of elimination until you feel like you have chosen the absolute correct answer. That's why the ten multiple-choice questions are so crucial on this test, even though they only account for ten of the 48 points. Unlike the Reading OGT, where you are often asked to infer or to make judgments about concepts that are not there on the page, most of the multiple-choice questions on this test are very straightforward and logical. Let's take a look.

A common way to test your revision skills will be to give you a sentence and ask you the correct way to revise or edit it without changing the meaning. Right there you can eliminate any of the four choices that *do* change the meaning of the given sentence. Then look for anything about the sentence that's vague or unclear. There may not be anything incorrect grammatically about the sentence that's to be revised, or it may be something that seems obvious such as capitalizing the name of a proper noun.

Another type of revision that's tested in Writing Processes is how to revise a paragraph. You will be given a numbered paragraph and asked such questions as the correct way to revise one of its sentences. This may be asking you to make a sentence with passive voice more active (we'll discuss that later) or to rearrange the words so that it's more clear and understandable. It may also be asking you to correct a misplaced modifier or dangling participle. Don't worry—those sound scary, but after we review and practice correcting them, you'll spot them a mile away and have no trouble.

Other questions in this section might ask what to include or what not to include in a certain paragraph. Also, you may be asked about the steps in the writing process or the best sentence to use to open or close a paragraph or essay.

One of the more interesting types of questions in this section involves giving you a set of rules about grammar and then asking you to answer a question that puts those rules in action. These should seem very easy to you as long as you read them carefully. Even though this is the Writing OGT, you have to go slowly and be willing to read the questions carefully. Keep in mind that for this type of question, if you take your time, you should be nearly guaranteed to spot the correct answer—the rules are right there for you. Students who miss these typically do so because they rush or take the question too lightly. Don't forget that there are only ten of these multiple-choice questions, so you'll want to get them all correct.

Sometimes you can be asked about how to organize your ideas, such as using a planner, chart, graph, or what can be classified as a "graphic organizer." Other questions might involve what resources to consult for a particular use, such as a dictionary, thesaurus, almanac, encyclopedia, and so on.

The short-answer question on the Writing OGT will be one that asks you to do some writing in the answer booklet. There are not two different scales for this question; it will simply be graded out of two points. Look for the question to spell out for you that two different ideas are required. You may be asked, for example, to compose two ideas to share at a public event where you are proposing a new land development. If they ask for two ideas, make sure you give them two. Make sure also that the two ideas answer the question specifically and are not two different ways to say the same thing. For your short answer, you may be given some ideas to organize into a paragraph. Treat this like a puzzle: You must put the pieces in the right places. Remember to use the same concepts that you used when you answered revision questions in the multiple-choice section. Good writing, after all, is good writing.

Try to answer this question, making sure to provide the correct information:

> Your school district is considering having school on Saturday and having students attend school six days a week. You are planning to address the Board of Education about this. Write two arguments that you would use to support or oppose this.

Just for practice, let's list three ideas to support and three to oppose.

SUPPORT:

1 _____

_____

2 _____

_____

3 _____

_____

OPPOSE

1 _____

2 _____

3 _____

You probably mentioned in the support section that 1) students could learn more if they went to school 6 days, 2) this would allow students to graduate in fewer than four years, and 3) students could have a longer summer break. And to oppose, 1) this would interfere with family plans and student activities, 2) students need time to relax and process what they have learned in a full week, and 3) this would also be disruptive to the families of teachers and other school employees.

You'll notice that each of those ideas does answer the question, and that for each you would have been able in a sentence or two to explain the idea.

Let's take a closer look at some of the standards in this section and what they might look like on the test.

QUESTIONS ABOUT THESIS STATEMENTS

A thesis statement is the sentence that tells the reader what your essay or composition will be about—it's the road map to an essay. It also directly answers the question that you are asked to address. The thesis statement usually is the last sentence in your introduction. Which one of these sentences looks like it could be a thesis statement?

  A. I rode my bike all afternoon.

  B. Even though we lost, the championship game was a great learning experience.

  C. The motorcycle was the fastest machine I had ever seen.

  D. That was when I realized my mistake.

Can you tell that three of those are more like details, even though they could appear in any essay? The only one that seems to be a way to tell the reader what the essay will be about is B. It tells the reader that you will be describing a championship game that you lost, but that it was a great learning experience.

WRITING FOR AN AUDIENCE

Any time you write, think about your audience. Your writing audience is no different from an audience at a play or concert—it is who is there listening. Like a musical concert, the performer will want to sing or play what the audience wants to hear and likes to hear. In writing, it's about what language to use and how to help the audience understand your ideas.

An easy way to make sure you consider your audience is to remember the acronym SOAPS. This stands for Subject, Occasion, Audience, Purpose, Speaker. If you think through these elements, it will help you to focus your response so it not only answers the question but does it in a way that's effective and appropriate as well.

Your audience in an English class is usually your teacher. Sometimes you may be asked in class to write to the principal or to the Board of Education. How might that change your writing? You might use more formal language, avoid slang, and not be quite as "friendly" in how you phrase your ideas. How about if you were writing a pamphlet for elementary school students? How would that change how you write? Let's try it.

> Choose the best way to revise the following sentence for an elementary school audience.
>
> When you get to middle school, it will be crucial for you to spend the appropriate amount of time on your academic studies.
>
> A. Middle school is harder than elementary school.
> B. In middle school, you must make sure to spend enough time studying and learning.
> C. You will not have as much free time in middle school.
> D. Many students do not do as well in middle school as in elementary school.

So what did you think needed to change about the sample sentence? It was a little too wordy, right? And there were a couple of words that might have been too sophisticated for younger children, like "crucial" and "academic." On the other hand, choice A is too simple and loses the meaning of the sentence. Options C and D also simplify but change the meaning of what the sample sentence was trying to say. Choice B then does the trick—it simplifies but conveys the same meaning.

USING PARAGRAPH FORM

You've been writing paragraphs for years, but the older you get, the better you get at using language. Sometimes it can be easy to forget that there is a definite structure to how to put together a paragraph. Let's review the organization of a standard paragraph.

Topic Sentences

A paragraph begins with a topic sentence. Your essay has a thesis statement that gives direction to the writing, and the topic sentence is like the thesis for the paragraph— it tells the reader what to expect in that paragraph. If the paragraph is part of a larger essay, the topic sentence should relate back in some way to the thesis of the essay.

In a paragraph about your summer vacation, which of the following sentences would be a good topic sentence?

A. Swimming at the beach all day was fun.
B. Have you ever wanted to play baseball?
C. The best part of summer was our trip to Mexico.
D. When summer ended, I was ready to go back to school.

Think about which sentence would be a good beginning sentence for a paragraph that will describe your summer vacation. They might all have something to do with summer, but notice how C is set up to allow you to describe your summer vacation, as the question asked. It's best in many ways because it is clear and specific. That is how you want to write topic sentences.

Concrete Details

Once you have introduced your paragraph with a topic sentence, you must describe what you want to say with concrete details. Why do you think they are called concrete? Think about using details and examples that are solid and that you could see or touch. That way, you will be sure the reader understands what you are trying to say or prove. Let's try a method for making sure to use concrete details. Think of this technique as "doubling."

Write a descriptive sentence about your favorite TV show.

_____

Now double the amount of writing you used to describe the show.

_____

_____

Now double that amount.

_____

_____

_____

Does yours look like this?

1. *American Idol* is a singing competition.
2. *American Idol* is a singing competition where people from all over the country try out for a chance to be famous.
3. *American Idol* is a singing competition where people from all over the country try out for a chance to be famous in hopes that they can win a recording contract and become a singing superstar like the winners of the show who came before them.

See how it works? See how sentence 3 is much more informative and interesting than sentence 2? You may not have thought there was anything wrong with sentence 1 (or your first sentence). But this isn't about right and wrong. Think of it as being more convincing and interesting. When it comes to details and examples, it's not likely that you can be too descriptive, as long as you don't repeat yourself.

Transitions

You will want to use transitions in your paragraphs between your details and examples. This helps your writing to be more clear and smooth. There are many different transitions you can use, depending on what you are saying in your paragraph. Here is a good list to consider:

Transitions that can be used to show **time**:

while	first	meanwhile	soon	then
after	second	today	later	next
at	third	tomorrow	afterward	as soon as
before	now	next week	about	when suddenly
during	until	yesterday	finally	

Transitions that can be used to **compare**:

| likewise | also | while | in the same way |
| like | as | similarly | |

Transitions that can be used to **contrast** two ideas:

| but | still | although | on the other hand |
| however | yet | otherwise | even though |

Transitions that can be used to **emphasize a point**:

| again | truly | especially | for this reason |
| to repeat | in fact | to emphasize | |

Transitions that can be used to **conclude or summarize**:

| finally | as a result | to sum up | in conclusion |
| lastly | therefore | all in all | because |

Transitions that can be used to **add information**:

again	another	for instance	for example
also	and	moreover	additionally
as well	besides	along with	other
next	finally	in addition	

Transitions that can be used to **clarify**:

| that is | for instance | in other words |

Think about your TV show descriptive sentences. Imagine that you were going to continue that paragraph, and choose four transitions from the list of samples. Write them below.

_____ _____

_____ _____

For a descriptive paragraph it's likely you would use transitions like "for example," "additionally," and "moreover." You may also want to use emphasis transitions, such as "for this reason" and "in fact." Note that they are not interchangeable; make sure the transitions match the reason you are using them.

Concluding Sentence

Just like your essay needs a conclusion, your paragraph needs a concluding sentence. This will summarize the main ideas in the paragraph and provides an end point, telling the reader you are finished with your thoughts. It should not introduce any new ideas.

Which of the following sentences would be an appropriate way to conclude that summer vacation paragraph we talked about earlier?

A. We did a lot of other fun things on vacation, too.
B. I swam for several hours that first day.
C. After seeing all of the amazing sites, I can't wait to visit Mexico again.
D. We were in Mexico for eight days total.

If you think about what would have been described in that paragraph, then you can see that choice A is introducing new ideas, which is not what we want the concluding sentence to do. B and D are too specific and don't properly conclude the paragraph. Choice C summarizes the paragraph and gives it a "done" feeling.

Try writing a concluding sentence for a paragraph you might write about your favorite TV show

_____

_____

Does it add new information? Does it attempt to summarize? Does it give the reader the feeling that you are finished with the paragraph?

You will be asked questions about revising on the Writing OGT, but they will be in the form of multiple-choice questions. According to the standard, there are many reasons you may want to revise your writing. Let's walk though a sample.

Read the draft paragraph below and answer the question that follows.

1. Ohio has many fun places to go if you want to see interesting things that don't cost a fortune. 2. Art and music can be found in some. 3. Others offer people good food. 4. Swimming, boating, and fishing are common at the lakes in Ohio. 5. These places are fun to visit.

In the context of the paragraph, what is the correct way to revise sentence 2?

A. Around the state can be found art and music.
B. Art and music can be found at some.
C. At some can be found art and music.
D. Some of the attractions have art and music.

So you might be looking at sentence 2 and thinking, "It looks okay to me." You'd be correct in thinking that there is nothing truly wrong with it. But in revision questions, you are asked to make the sentence better. Choice D is the most clear and concise way to revise sentence 2. The other choices are either awkwardly worded or use what we call passive voice. Avoid using passive voice, such as "can be found," because it is vague and unclear (who did the finding?). We will discuss passive voice in more detail in Chapter 11.

Chapter 8 Wrap-Up

Chapter 8 was all about Writing Processes; that is, the process of writing. You've leaning how to write well for years, and this standard will ask you to show what you know.

- Many of the OGT questions that test this standard will be multiple choice, so follow what you have learned about how to be successful on tests such as these.

- For questions that give you rules and ask you to apply them to sample sentences, smile. All you have to do to get those correct is read carefully and take your time.

- For revision questions, don't look for errors. Think about how the choices sound or which are more clear, less confusing, or better aligned with the subject.

- When it comes to paragraph structure, think about past essays you have written for English class or other subject areas. Remember where the paragraph parts belong and what the purpose of each part is.

- Make sure to avoid using text message language in your writing, such as b/c, idk, and others. Even if you think the reader will know what you mean, use your best and most specific grammar and diction (word choice) in your writing.

Writing Applications

THE STANDARD

1. Write narratives that:
   a. sustain reader interest by pacing action and developing an engaging plot (e.g., tension and suspense);
   b. use a range of strategies and literary devices including figurative language and specific narration;
   c. include an organized, well-developed structure.
2. Write responses to literature that organize an insightful interpretation around several clear ideas, premises or images and support judgments with specific references to the original text, to other texts, authors and to prior knowledge.
3. Write business letters, letters to the editor and job applications that:
   a. address audience needs, stated purpose and context in a clear and efficient manner;
   b. follow the conventional style appropriate to the text using proper technical terms;
   c. include appropriate facts and details;
   d. exclude extraneous details and inconsistencies; and
   e. provide a sense of closure to the writing.
4. Write informational essays or reports, including research that:
   a. pose relevant and tightly drawn questions that engage the reader;
   b. provide a clear and accurate perspective on the subject;
   c. create an organizing structure appropriate to the purpose, audience and context;
   d. support the main ideas with facts, details, examples and explanations from sources; and
   e. document sources and include bibliographies.
5. Write persuasive compositions that:
   a. establish and develop a controlling idea;
   b. support arguments with detailed evidence;
   c. exclude irrelevant information; and
   d. cite sources of information.
6. Produce informal writings (e.g., journals, notes and poems) for various purposes.

Y ou'll note that in this standard, benchmark 2 involves responding to literature. It's unlikely that you be asked to complete this type of response, as it would involve giving you a passage to read, which is more appropriate on the Reading OGT. Also, benchmark 4 involves doing actual research on a topic and using sources in your composition, so it's unlikely that you'd be asked to complete a piece of writing like that on this test. Benchmark 6 could certainly be accomplished on a test like this, but it would be rather difficult to evaluate such writing using the Writing Process and Writing Conventions scales, so don't count on being asked to complete those types of informal writing on the Writing OGT either.

That leaves us with narrative (story), informational (expository) without research, and persuasive writing. Note that other than the narrative, you could also be asked to put these in the form of a letter, which is benchmark 3.

Let's break down the different types of writing you might be asked to do so that you're clear on the different parts that must be included.

NARRATIVE OR STORY WRITING

Part of the goal of meeting the standard of a good story is developing the plot. A typical plotline of a story has the following parts:

Exposition: This is the beginning where you set the scene, introduce the characters, and start to explain the situation.

Rising Action: This is where the characters might begin to struggle or begin to face obstacles or conflicts. This builds up interest on the part of the reader.

Climax: This is the high point of the story. All of the Rising Action has built up to this moment and the reader is very interested to see what he or she has been waiting for.

Falling Action: This is where things start to settle a bit in the story after the excitement of the Climax. It's not quite the end, but you can tell that things are starting to wind down.

Resolution: This is the part at the end where everything gets worked out or at least you explain to the reader how everything ends up for all of the characters who were involved in the story.

That all seems pretty logical, doesn't it? Let's see if you can identify which parts of the story are which. Fill in the name of the part of the story next to the example.

_____ 1. The boy and girl began to like each other.

_____ 2. After the date, they decided to continue to talk a lot.

_____ 3. A boy and a girl met each other in English class.

_____ 4. On their date, they had a great time and lots of fun.

_____ 5. They fell in love and lived happily ever after.

Did you find the Exposition? It's #3, when they first met. How about the Rising Action? That's when they begin to get to know each other, so #1. The Climax is the fun date, #4. Falling Action in this example is #2, because it's after the date. And the Resolution had a corny giveaway—it's #5 with "happily ever after."

In addition to writing a story with all parts of the plot present, you must also think about how to narrate it. You can use 1st person, which means you will be a part of the story and use words like *I* and *me*. This allows you to be very specific and descriptive, but you can only know what your character knows.

Think about characterization, too. That is, who will be the characters in your story, and how will you make them come alive for the reader? You can use direct characterization, in which you describe a character and tell the reader his or her qualities, such as quiet, sensitive, hot-tempered, and other physical descriptions. You can also use indirect characterization, which is letting the reader know about a character by how the character acts and talks, or by how the other characters in the story react to him or her.

You may want to use 3rd person omniscient. Think back to the Reading OGT practice section on vocabulary. *Omni* means "all," and *scien* means "knowing." This type of narration means that you are "all-knowing." You can talk about what all of the characters are thinking and feeling, and you can know what all of the characters are doing at all times. This is a less personal way to tell the story, but it allows you to talk about more things and add more detail.

Finally, you must make sure your story is well organized and well developed. The plot elements should help with this, but you should also spend time doing some prewriting using the space provided in the test booklet. Some students don't like to take time to prewrite, but you should know that it can only help. It is likely that you will have plenty of time for this test, so there is no hurry. Think about using some sort of graphic organizer such as a web or chart. This will ensure that you complete the story with all the right parts. Also make sure to develop each part. Think about explaining what's happening in your story with as much detail as you can. Let's practice this with a sample prompt.

> Think about a time when something scary happened to you. Write a story about such a time. Make sure your story includes details about what was scary, how you reacted, and how everything ended up.

Sounds like a pretty easy task, and you could probably rattle off a decent story without planning or prewriting. But let's see how much easier it is and how much more organized we can be by taking time to plan.

Based on the prompt, it seems like 1st person is the choice for narration style, since they asked about "you."

Describe the setting (time, place, location) of your story in which something scary happened:

_____

_____

Describe what exactly was scary about this situation:

_____

_____

Describe what you said or did:

_____

_____

Describe how this situation ended:

_____

_____

Just this amount of planning will make your story better. If you describe the parts above, then your story will have detail and development. Now let's make sure your story has all the required parts. Briefly fill in the plot elements:

Exposition: _____

_____

Rising Action: _____

_____

Climax: _____

_____

Falling Action: _____

_____

Resolution: _____

_____

Now you can be sure that you have all the parts and you know what types of details to include for your story to be considered well-developed. The rest is just stringing them together in order, using the right words, and using correct grammar. That's still a lot to keep in mind, but for now you have "your story straight"!

See if you can label the following parts of this sample story:

1. I will never forget the night that I took the dare and went into the abandoned hospital. It was a Halloween night, and we were bored, so we went over to the gates of the hospital and talked about what it might look like inside. It was very dark and creepy that night, so all of our thoughts kept us on edge.

2. Things really started to get tense when John noticed that the lock on the gate was broken and pushed it open, making the most hideous shrieking sound ever. I couldn't believe it, but then he actually walked though the gate and started walking toward the front doors of the hospital. It all seemed like a bad movie.

3. I don't know why, but I decided to follow him to the door. I guess I didn't want to look like a chicken. The whole way there I was worried that something bad would happen. I was right. Just as we reached the door, very bright lights lit up the entire area. We nearly jumped out of our skin. It was the police, and they had been notified that there were trespassers at the old hospital.

4. I remember feeling so silly as they put us in the back of the police cruiser. John looked sorry that he had done it, but there was the hint of a smile on his face like he still thought it had been fun.

5. The police called our parents and they had to come pick us up at the police station. It was very embarrassing, but in the end no one got hurt and I learned a valuable lesson about going with something that didn't seem right.

What paragraph is the Exposition? _____

Rising Action? _____

Climax? _____

Falling Action? _____

Resolution? _____

Not too tough here, because it moves just like it should: 1, 2, 3, 4, 5. Hopefully seeing it in paragraphs shows you the logical way the story progresses and that it does have all the parts of a good story.

INFORMATIONAL WRITING (EXPOSITORY)

This type of writing for the purposes of the Writing OGT will be to relay or "expose" information to the reader. Since you can't use research, the composition will be your ideas explained to the reader in response to the question you are asked. You are simply presenting ideas with explanations to the reader. You might, for example, be asked to describe a principle or moral in which you strongly believe. All you have to do is explain why you feel strongly that you choose to live your life by this moral or principle. You are not being asked to write a story with different parts, a letter to anyone, or to persuade the reader that he or she should live the same way. Simply answer the question you are asked. You will still want to be organized and have several reasons that explain why you feel the way you do. Also, you will still want to develop your composition with specific, concrete details. And, of course, you'll want to use MUGS (mechanics, usage, grammar, spelling). Let's try to plan this one out using a web.

In the center circle below, put the main idea, or the principle/moral by which you live your life.

Fill in three of the outer circles with reasons that support your choice. Make sure they are different reasons and not the same reasons stated with different words.

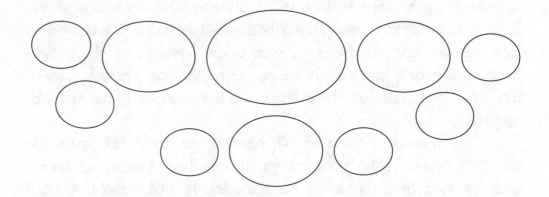

Take a look at what you wrote. Is the middle bubble your main answer to the question? If so, you are in good shape. The outer bubbles are your main reasons in support of the main idea; they become your paragraphs. Don't have too many. Three is a decent guideline.

In the next outer set of bubbles, add some details to describe your reasons. Add two details for each reason. As a rule of thumb, if you only have one detail to support a reason, it might not be such a good reason. Perhaps it would be better off in a different part of the piece of writing. That's the value of prewriting—it allows you to see all of this ahead of time and to make adjustments. That's not very easy once you start writing and are forced to erase.

PERSUASIVE WRITING

Everyone is persuasive from time to time, perhaps even every day. When you care about something, it's easy to be persuasive. You just say what you feel. For the Writing OGT, if you can imagine that the Writing Prompts are real, you might actually find that they are easier to write.

Persuasion is divided into three categories known as rhetoric. They have fancy Greek names, but it's far more important that you are able to use all three types effectively than it is to remember their names.

Ethos: This is an appeal to the reader's sense of ethics, such as their integrity and his or her sense of right and wrong.

Logos: This is an appeal to the reader's sense of logic. You may try to make things very step-by-step and scientific for the the reader. Use of statistics is common here.

Pathos: This is an appeal to the emotion of the reader. You can try to tap into his or her sense of love, anger, fear, or other strong emotions.

Using these three appeals depends on both the topic of your argument and your audience. For example, if you were speaking to a group of scientists, which appeal sounds most effective? Logos, right? Scientists rely on facts and evidence, so it stands to reason that they would be persuaded by logic. How about a group of new moms? This might be the time for pathos. We can assume that new moms are likely to be protective of their newborn babies, and they could be persuaded by appealing to their emotions. Who might be likely to be persuaded by ethos? People who are highly ethical themselves or who occupy positions of ethics, such as priests, soldiers, or event teachers and doctors, right? All of these people serve as public role models and are expected to have high moral values and ethics.

Another technique used in persuasion is called Refuting the Opposition. In this technique, you mention or acknowledge part of the other side of the argument, but then you refute it or tell why there are problems with it. This strengthens your argument. It also tells the reader you are both aware of the other side and are not afraid to mention it. Obviously, you don't want to talk too much about the other side or bring up parts of their argument that are so strong you can't refute them.

Let's practice constructing a persuasive argument using a practice prompt.

> Your family has just won a large sum of money in the lottery but the catch is that you can only spend it in one place or in one way. Each family member was asked to submit a proposal for how to spend the money. Write a proposal to your parents persuading them how/where they should spend the money.

Write out your argument for how/where they should spend the money:

_____

_____

Describe one reason for this that appeals to ethics (ethos):

_____

_____

Describe one reason for this that appeals to emotion (pathos):

_____

_____

Describe one reason for this that appeals to logic (logos):

_____

_____

Describe one reason for the opposition (a reason other than yours):

_____

_____

Refute the opposition (describe why their reason is poor/yours is better):

_____

_____

Those are all the steps to a persuasive argument. Like all of the other compositions, you must be organized and develop your ideas with specific, concrete examples. You must also use correct MUGS. We will cover those in the next chapter on Writing Conventions.

Let's finish Writing Processes with some talk and practice on writing letters, as you may be asked to do this for one of the Writing Prompts. If you look back at the standard, you will see that some of what you must keep in mind are the parts of a letter and the audience.

For the parts of a letter, you must have a greeting, a body, and a closing. Common greetings are "To Whom It May Concern" or one tailored to the prompt, such as "Dear Scholarship Committee." The body of your letter will be the paragraphs that answer the specific question. Each paragraph should have a clear purpose. The closing is similar to the greeting in that it should match the audience. "Sincerely" is very common and matches almost any audience. "Love" is reserved for very friendly audiences or family. If you are addressing a politician, the president, or someone else in a formal position, you can make your closing more formal, such as "Respectfully" or "With Sincere Gratitude."

Addressing your audience also means deciding what types of words and phrases to use. You can speak more conversationally to your friends and family than you can to your city's mayor or to the principal of your local college or university. Avoid slang phrases in those more formal letters and follow all rules of politeness and proper etiquette.

See if you can spot the different parts of the following sample letter:

Dear Mr. Smith,

I am a student at Jones Middle School, and I am writing to let you know how much I enjoyed your presentation on Careers in the Medical Field.

I would like to go to college to be a doctor, so everything you talked about was very useful to me.

Thank you again for coming and for sharing your advice with us. It was much appreciated.

Sincerely,

Jenny Brown

You can see that it begins with a greeting—a pretty formal one since the letter is to an adult. They body consists of two paragraphs about why she is writing the letter and offering her appreciation. Finally, she closes the letter appropriately with "Sincerely," and her name.

Chapter 9 Wrap-Up

This chapter focused on what you are writing and how you approach the task.

- You should be prepared for any of the types of writing that you may be asked to do: narrative, expository, or persuasive.

- You should also be prepared to put your writing in the form of a letter. Remember to consider your audience.

- No matter what you are asked to write, keep in mind that each type of writing has different parts that must be included.

Writing Conventions

THE STANDARD

1. Use correct spelling conventions.

2. Use correct capitalization and punctuation.

3. Use clauses (e.g., main, subordinate) and phrases (e.g., gerund, infinitive, participial).

4. Use parallel structure to present items in a series and items juxtaposed for emphasis.

5. Use proper placement of modifiers.

6. Maintain the use of appropriate verb tenses.

> Spelling

> Punctuation and Capitalization

> Grammar and Usage

This one is pretty short and sweet, but it involves some of the finer points of grammar that are difficult for many students. Part of what might make it seem tougher are the names of the parts of grammar. Let's break some of that down before we get too much further.

Correct Spelling Conventions: No tricks here. "Conventions" just means that you follow the rules of spelling. Easy.

Correct Capitalization and Punctuation: This refers to when to capitalize and when not to. We will review those rules later, but you also might have already been tested on them in the multiple-choice section. We will also review punctuation, which simply refers to commas, periods, quotation marks, and other such items you have used often.

Use Clauses and Phrases: This one sounds a bit scarier, especially if you haven't had a lot of grammar study in your English classes. In this chapter you'll learn how to think of these in a much less intimidating way, and you will be able to use clauses and phrases effectively and correctly.

Clauses: A clause is a group of words with a subject and a predicate.

- A main clause expresses a complete thought.

    He went to the store.

- A subordinate clause does not express a complete thought and can't stand on its own without a main clause.

    because he wanted to buy milk.

Notice that the subordinate clause would need the main clause to make a complete sentence.

Phrases: Phrases are a group of related words without a verb.

- A gerund phrase is formed from a verb but acts as a noun.

    <u>Paying bills</u> is not fun.

By itself, "paying" can be a verb. Because it is acting as the subject of this sentence, it's considered a gerund.

- An infinitive phrase is the word "to" plus a verb.

    He likes <u>to run</u>.

These are also formed with verbs, but like gerunds, infinitives are not used as verbs. Infinitives are used as nouns, adjectives, or adverbs.

- A participial phrase is formed using a verb with an *–ing* ending. Participial phrases are used as adjectives, even though they might look like gerunds.

    The <u>setting</u> sun was pretty.

We'll practice these concepts more later, but that should help you to see that you use these elements all the time in your writing, and you will continue to use them on your compositions for the Writing OGT and throughout your life. Don't let the names bother you; we'll practice how to write well and with an interesting style and voice, which will involve you using those clauses and phrases naturally.

SPELLING

This comes naturally to many people, and sometimes practice is the only way to get better. Let's review some common rules and common errors, though, that will help you brush up on spelling.

Rule 1: *i* before *e* except after *c* or when it sounds like *a*.

    Example: relieve (*i* before *e*)
                    receive (except after *c*)
                    neighbor (or when it sounds like *a*)

Rule 2: What to do with final *e*'s.

- If the suffix or ending you're adding begins with a vowel, drop the *e*.

  amuse + ing = amusing

- If the suffix begins with a consonant, keep the *e*.

  amuse + ment = amusement

Rule 3: If you have a word ending in *y* then . . .

- If the word has a consonant before the *y*, change the *y* to *i*.

  mercy + less = merciless

- If the word has a vowel before the *y*, keep the *y*.

  employ + ment = employment

Rule 4: Plurals

- Words that end in *ss*, *sh*, *ch* or *x* add *es*.

  match = matches

- Words that have a consonant before a final *y*, change the *y* to *i* before adding *es*.

  summary = summaries

- Most nouns ending in *f* or *fe* add *s*. However, some change the *f* to *v* and add *s* or *es*.

  belief = beliefs; half = halves

- Most nouns ending in *o* add *s*. However, some add *es*.

  studio = studios; hero = heroes

Rule 5: The spelling of a word does not change when you add a prefix to it even when the first letter of the word and the last letter of the prefix are the same.

  mis + step = misstep

  un + necessary = unnecessary

CAPITALIZATION AND PUNCTUATION REVIEW

Most of these are rules you know already, but let's review them in case there are any you aren't sure of or have confused. There are examples provided for some of these rules; for others, there is a blank for you to use to fill in your own example.

Capitalization Rules

- Capitalize the beginning of a sentence.

_____

- Capitalize the pronoun "I."

_____

- Capitalize proper nouns: specific people, places, and organizations

    The National Council of Teachers of English has a convention every year.

- Capitalize religious figures, holy books, and God.

    They quoted *Genesis* in the sermon.

- Capitalize days of the week, holidays, and months of the year <u>but not seasons</u>.

_____

- Capitalize countries, languages, and nationalities.

    The Germans spoke German in Germany.

- Capitalize family relationships only when used instead of proper names.

    My dad is nice, and Mother is nice, too.

- Capitalize titles that precede names, but not titles that follow names.

    The governor called up President Bush.

- Capitalize North, South, East, and West when used as sections of the country, but not as compass directions.

_____

- Capitalize letter salutations and closings.

_____

- Capitalize major words in titles of books, written works, or songs.

    [Short definite or indefinite articles (*the, a,* or *an*) are not capitalized if they aren't the first word.]

    My favorite book is _____.

- Capitalize events and periods of time.

    Of Mice and Men takes place during the Depression.

- Capitalize company product names.

- Capitalize words and abbreviations of specific names.

  His dad was a member of the NRA.

- Capitalize names of planets in the solar system.

You probably did well on those. Now let's look at punctuation. Review the following common rules and make sure you know all the tricks and exceptions. Examples are given for the more complex rules.

Punctuation

Period

- Use a period at the end of a sentence, after an initial, and after an abbreviation.

Exclamation Point

- Use an exclamation point at the end of sentence to indicate strong emotion.

Question Mark

- Use a question mark at the end of a question.

Comma

- Use a comma after each item in a series of at least three items, after the street address and city in an address, but not after the state.

- Use a comma after the day and the year in a date within a sentence.

- Use a comma to separate two or more adjectives that describe the same noun.

  The day was cold, rainy, and wet.

- Use a comma after a subordinate clause that begins a sentence.

  When I arrived home, I took a nap.

- Use a comma before the conjunction in a compound sentence.

  I slept for hours, and then I woke up and had a snack.

- When using quotation marks, put a comma inside the quotation marks.

  "Take out the trash," his brother yelled.

- Use a comma after the greeting in a personal letter.

- Use a comma after the closing of a letter.

Semicolon

- Use a semicolon to join two independent clauses.

    The movie was over at midnight; they called for a ride home.

Colon

- Use a colon to introduce a list.

    The following students should report to the office for the raffle: John, Mary, and Jill.

- Use a colon after the greeting of a business letter.

Apostrophe

- Use an apostrophe in a contraction to show where letters have been left out.

    Don't tell her what I said.

- If a plural noun ends in *-s*, add an apostrophe after the *-s*.

    The boys' bus arrived. (This refers to more than one boy.)
    The boy's bus arrived. (This refers to one boy.)

Quotation Marks

- Use quotation marks before and after a direct quote.

    The teacher said, "Pass up your homework."

- Put quotation marks around the titles of articles, songs, short stories, or poems.

Underlining

- Underline titles of books, magazines, CDs, movies, and plays.

CLAUSES

Let's take a closer look at main and subordinate clauses.

Remember that a main clause has a subject and a predicate or verb. But it must be able to stand by itself. If not, it is considered a fragment in writing—a major error showing that one does not understand the rules of writing. One way to tell if you've written a fragment is to read the main clause out loud to determine if it is a complete thought.

For example, if you read the following series of words, you will see how it leaves you waiting for the rest of the story:

After he went to the store.

It looks like a sentence, and it even has a subject and a verb. The first word, though, makes it a subordinate clause. It does not express a complete thought, and it cannot stand by itself.

PARALLEL STRUCTURE

This concept is designed so that your writing is consistent, especially if you are listing more than one example of something in a sentence. Here are some examples:

Not Parallel: John likes hik*ing,* swimm*ing,* and *to ride* a bicycle.

Parallel: John likes hik*ing,* swimm*ing,* and rid*ing* a bicycle.

In the first sentence above, there are gerunds used and then an infinitive. (If you're still learning these names, that's okay.) You can tell just by looking at the sentence and listening to it that the third element, the infinitive, is different. All three verbs in this sentence should match, or be parallel, as shown in the second sentence.

Try filling in a parallel word in the second sentence below to correct the problem in the first sentence:

Not Parallel: The production manager was asked to write his report quick*ly,* accurate*ly,* and *in a detailed manner.*

Parallel: The production manager was asked to write his report quick*ly,* accurate*ly,* and _____.

You can see that we have a series of adverbs to describe how the production manager was asked to write her report. It ends in a prepositional phrase, though. What did you fill in? Hopefully, an *ly* adverb! The words *professionally* or *thoroughly* would work well. If you didn't use an *ly* adverb, it's likely that you just traded one parallel structure problem for another, so be careful and check your work.

One other aspect of Writing Conventions that's worth reviewing is the use of modifiers.

Misplaced Modifier: Words such as *only, just, nearly,* and *barely* can be used in the wrong place in a sentence and be unclear.

He barely hit the ball fifty feet.

He hit the ball barely fifty feet.

In this example, it's unclear if the focus is on the distance or how hard he hit the ball.

Dangling Modifier: If you begin a sentence with a phrase that modifies or describes, you must make sure the word that follows it is what it's describing.

Making very poor decisions, the car was driven recklessly.

In this case, we have a participial phrase that makes it appear that the car is making decisions. This is corrected by making the sentence more active.

Making very poor decisions, the man drove the car recklessly.

Directions: Try correcting the dangling modifiers in the following sentences.

Spending way too much money on her music, Cindy's salary just wasn't enough.

_____

_____

Swinging wildly through the trees, the children were delighted by the monkeys.

_____

_____

The first sentence should be corrected to something like this:

Spending way too much money on her music, Cindy realized that her salary just wasn't enough.

Notice that the subject, <u>Cindy</u>, had to follow the opening modifying phrase.

For the second sentence, did you see how important it is to correct? The way it reads right now, the children are "swinging wildly through the trees." Here's the correction:

Swinging wildly through the trees, the monkeys delighted the children.

You may have noticed that many of these problems are caused by using the passive voice. Let's take a look at how to avoid using passive voice.

Here's an easy and fun way to remember this concept:

Active Voice: Why did the chicken cross the road?

Passive Voice: Why was the road crossed by the chicken?

If you think that both of these questions say the same thing, you're right. If you think that both of them are grammatically correct, you're right, again. If you think that both are equally clear and interesting, then many would disagree. And as mentioned above, passive voice causes problems in writing, so let's practice avoiding it.

Directions: Rewrite the following passive voice sentences into active voice:

John was introduced by Suzy.

_____

The ball was caught by the shortstop.

_____

The employees were informed by their boss that they were fired.

_____

_____

To correct "John was introduced by Suzy," you should have written "Suzy introduced John."

To correct "The ball was caught by the shortstop," you should have written "The shortstop caught the ball."

And "The employees were informed by their boss that they were fired," should be "The boss informed the employees that they were fired."

Not only will using active voice help you avoid some common grammatical errors, but it will also make your writing more interesting and enjoyable to read. That can do nothing except potentially raise your scores.

Chapter 10 Wrap-Up

The focus of this chapter was on the nuts and bolts of writing. You probably have been practicing all of these rules and techniques for years, so feel confident now that you have reviewed them and reminded yourself of some of the tricky exceptions and errors to avoid.

- Ideally, you will at some point learn all of the technical grammatical terms for all of this stuff, but it is not crucial in passing and scoring well on the Writing OGT. Don't get hung up on terminology; look at how the words are used and for what purpose. Trust your experience and your instincts.

- Many of these common errors can only be caught when you proofread, revise, and edit. Save time for that on test day; it's an important step.

Focus on Writing Skills for the Writing OGT

In this chapter, we will discuss how to produce writing on the OGT that will score high on the rubric. Some of this deals with style issues, and other parts involve avoiding common errors and avoiding damaging errors—that is, errors that will truly lower your score.

FOLLOW DIRECTIONS

I know what you're thinking. How can something so simple be such good advice? But year after year, students have lost points on assessments such as the Reading and Writing OGT not because they lacked knowledge or didn't perform well, but because they didn't take the time to *carefully* read the directions.

We've already addressed much of this earlier in this book, but let's review the most important places where directions are crucial.

1. **Short Answer:** Make sure you read the question carefully. Annotate or mark with your pencil the different parts of the question that you can identify. Most questions like this come in two parts: the "what?" and the "so what?" You can see that you must provide, for example, a detail and two reasons why it's accurate. So make sure to provide *two* reasons and that those reasons support the answer you give to the question.

2. **Writing Prompt (extended response):** We have already discussed how to put together responses to these questions that will score well. It bears repeating that the extended-response questions on the Reading OGT will likely spell out for you how to answer these questions and how many examples to give. For example, you might be asked to discuss how the author uses imagery, and list three examples from the text to support your answer. You have clearly been asked for four pieces of information there. Also, on the Reading OGT, you can use numbers and bullet points to help keep yourself organized. You should not do that on the Writing OGT, and in most cases, you will not be given a clear list of what to include. Be ready for different wording of the questions.

AVOID COMMON ERRORS

We covered the nitty-gritty specifics of grammar in Chapter 10, but some of the more common errors are easier to let slip into your writing and might even have the potential to lower your score.

Fragments and Run-ons

A sentence fragment is just what it sounds like—it's a piece of a sentence. When writing sentences, you want the whole thing and not just a piece. A run-on is also just what it sounds like—it's a sentence that runs on too long. Let's look at some examples and practice how to correct them.

Fragments are either missing a subject or a predicate, or they are subordinate clauses that are missing a main clause. Either way, it should be easy to spot them.

Fragment missing a subject: Ran down the street.
Correction: (add the subject) I ran down the street.

Fragment that is a subordinate clause: While I studied.
Correction: (add the main clause) While I studied, the TV was on. OR I studied while the TV was on.

Note that since a clause by definition has a subject and a verb, it may be tougher to spot. You will be able to tell by reading it that it is an incomplete thought, though.

Directions: Correct the following fragments.

1. Last night under the stars.

    _____

    _____

2. Although he liked pizza.

    _____

    _____

3. John, the owner's son.

    _____

    _____

4. Trying to find his way home.

_____

_____

5. Because she was the president.

_____

_____

There is more than one way to correct each of those, but here are some possible solutions that you might have used.

1. Last night under the stars, we listened to music.
2. Although he liked pizza, Austin ordered a salad instead.
3. John, the owner's son, worked all day Saturday.
4. Trying to find his way home, the dog walked along the street.
5. Because she was the president, Katie called the meeting to order.

Run-ons are a slightly different problem and require a different solution. A run-on occurs when you take two complete sentences or independent clauses and fuse or join them without separating the ideas. You may picture run-ons as being very long on the page, and many are. They don't have to be, though. Take a look at this example.

I went to the store I bought milk.

Looks pretty reasonable, but you'll notice that it has two main subjects and two main verbs. Having those two fused together like this makes it a run-on sentence. There are several ways to correct a run-on.

1. Make it two separate sentences.

   I went to the store. I bought milk.

2. Add a semi-colon.

   I went to the store; I bought milk.

3. Add a comma and a conjunction, such as *and, but,* or *or.*

   I went to the store, and I bought milk.

4. Remove the second subject and use a compound verb.

   I went to the store and bought milk.

Note: This only works if the two subjects are the same.

Subject-Verb Agreement

Most of the time, making subjects and verbs agree in number (singular and plural) is easy. There are a few tricky parts to this that we'll review now.

Here is a review of some of the rules:

- When the subject of a sentence is composed of two or more nouns or pronouns connected by *and*, use a plural verb.

    She and I are going to the movies.

- When two or more singular nouns or pronouns are connected by *or* or *nor*, use a singular verb.

    Either the book or the film is better.

- Do not be misled by a phrase that comes between the subject and the verb. The verb agrees with the subject, not with a noun or pronoun in the phrase.

    The boy who ran though the woods is tall.

    One of the doors is open.

- The words *each, each one, either, neither, everyone, everybody, anybody, anyone, nobody, somebody, someone*, and *no one* are singular and require a singular verb.

    Everyone should bring her book to class.

- Nouns such as *civics, mathematics, dollars, measles*, and *news* require singular verbs.

    The news was good today.

- Nouns such as *scissors, tweezers, trousers*, and *shears* require plural verbs. (There are two parts to these things.)

    The tweezers are under the sink.

- Collective nouns are words that imply more than one person but that are considered singular and take a singular verb, such as: *group, team, committee, class, and family.*

    The class is studying math.

Pronoun-Antecedent Reference

Here's another one that sounds scary but it really isn't. You use it all the time, and there are a few common errors that we will review so you can avoid them.

Every pronoun you write should refer clearly and unmistakably to one specific noun. We call this noun the *antecedent*. That antecedent must be *clear* and *unmistakable*. Antecedents must also agree in number. (The words *everybody, anybody, anyone, each, neither, nobody, someone* are singular and take singular pronouns.) And they must agree in gender or include "his or her."

Directions: Insert the correct pronoun for each of the following sentences.

1. A girl going to college should have no fears about _____ future.

2. Neither Bill nor _____ am responsible for this mess.

3. No one on this bus seems to know _____ way around this part of Columbus.

Let's see how you did. For #1, you need a female singular pronoun to match, so it should be *her.* For #2, you need a singular pronoun, and the verb given is "am," so you must use *I.* Sentence #3 must be singular and the gender is unknown, so it's best to use *his or her.* Most people would write *their* or would use that in speech, but it is not correct.

That's enough of this correcting errors and looking-out-for-exceptions-to-rules business. Let's get to the fun stuff: how to make your writing more interesting.

VARYING SENTENCE TYPES, LENGTHS, AND OPENINGS

There are four different types of sentences; try to use them all and a variety of each kind in your writing:

Simple sentence: a sentence with one independent clause and no subordinate clauses.

> He is a student.

Compound sentence: a sentence with multiple independent clauses but no subordinate clauses.

> He is a student, and he attends Smith High School.

Complex sentence: a sentence with one independent clause and at least one subordinate clause.

> After he attends high school, he plans to go to college.

Complex-Compound sentence: a sentence with multiple independent clauses and at least one subordinate clause.

> Although he is young, he plans to be a doctor, and he wants to be a surgeon.

Notice that there are small differences in these four types of sentences, but if you combine the four types, your writing will be much smoother and more interesting.

Now you try to create each of the four types of sentences. To check your work, label the dependent and subordinate clauses in each.

Simple: _____

Compound: _____

_____

Complex: _____

_____

Compound-Complex: _____

_____

_____

In addition to varying sentence types, also focus on beginning your sentence with different words. Vary the sentence openings, too. For example:

- begin with a subject

- begin with an adverb word

     first, thus, moreover, nevertheless, namely

- begin with a conjunctive phrase

     on the other hand, as a consequence, indeed

- begin with a prepositional phrase

     in the morning

- begin with a verbal phrase (for example, verb forms which do not function as verbs, like gerunds and participles);

- begin with an adjective phrase

     Tired and cranky

- begin with an absolute phrase

     Their sense of mischief awakened, the two boys plotted their next practical joke.

- begin with an adverb clause

     When I decided to attend college, . . .

- begin with an appositive (phrase that modifies or provides more information about the noun)

     A complex and intriguing book, *The Great Gatsby* is a common text read by high school juniors.

BE MINDFUL OF WORD CHOICE

The last concept to keep in mind as you fine tune your writing is to concentrate on using very vivid and descriptive details and examples. Try to remember the concept of "show, don't tell." This applies to any type of writing you are asked to do. For example, instead of saying something looked "nice," you could actually try to paint a mental picture for the reader by discussing colors, shapes, sizes, textures, and how it made you feel. Also, remember that words can have different meanings or connotations. Think of all the ways you can say a person is angry: mad, furious, miffed, peeved, upset, disgruntled. There are clearly many different ways, but each of them does not carry exactly the same shade of meaning. Are *mad* and *upset* the same? Probably not in your essay, so make sure you take care to choose the words that suit your sentence and essay best.

Scoring High on the Writing Prompt

We looked at the 6-point scale for Writing Applications in an earlier section, but let's focus in on how to earn a 6/6 on both evaluations of the piece. Here's the six-level rubric language again:

6 This is a superior piece of writing. The prompt is directly addressed, and the response is effectively adapted to audience and purpose. It is exceptionally developed, containing compelling ideas, examples and details. The response, using a clearly evident organizational plan, actively engages the reader with a unified and coherent sequence and structure of ideas. The response consistently uses a variety of sentence structures, effective word choices and an engaging style.

Breaking this down, you have the following elements:

1. Address the prompt exactly (answer the question!).
2. Address the audience and reflect the purpose of the task.
3. Develop your ideas and be organized.
4. Use specific examples and details that are convincing.
5. Use a variety of sentence types and use appropriate words.
6. Show some style and flair—some originality.

Now let's take a closer look at the 3-point Writing Conventions scale, specifically the 3/3 rubric language:

3 The written response is free from errors that impair a reader's understanding and comprehension. Few errors, if any, are present in capitalization, punctuation and spelling. The writing displays a consistent understanding of grammatical conventions.

Breaking that down, we see the following concepts:

1. Avoid serious errors that will keep the reader from understanding you.
2. Avoid errors that a tenth grader shouldn't make, such as errors in spelling, punctuation, and capitalization.
3. Show that you understand how to write correctly and in a variety of ways.

We have covered and practiced all of that already. Good writing should take concentration, planning, focus, and hard work. You'll get a chance to practice the real thing later in the practice test section, but for now, take a look at a response that would have scored a 6/6 on the 6-point scale and a 3/3 on the 3-point Writing Conventions scale using a very common type of prompt:

> Some students believe that colleges look too closely at the applicants' cumulative grade point averages. For example, some colleges claim that they will not admit students who do not have, say, at least a 3.5 GPA on a 4.0 scale. State and defend your position on this issue to an audience of college admissions officers. Be sure to include specific reasons in support of your position. Write your response in the Answer Document. (18 points).

Note: As a reminder, the essay is scored on the 6-point Writing Applications scale and the 3-point Writing Conventions scale by two different readers. The total possible points, then, is 18.

College admissions policies that require a minimum GPA are inappropriate and unfair. This system must be changed. As it stands now, quality students all over the country are being unfairly kept from expanding their minds with higher education, and this system that puts such a high value on grade point averages is clearly to blame. This is not simply a hindrance to the future success of high school students—this affects the future of the entire country and perhaps the world.

I understand why colleges use a student's GPA as a measure. It is supposed to be an equal measure of student performance and be a strong indication of how a student will fare in college. This is partially valid; however, what most high school students will tell you is that their GPA, even if it's very high, is not an accurate measure of their intellect or of their abilities. If students with high GPAs are saying this, then we can assume that it's true, as they have no reason not to be truthful.

Furthermore, penalizing a student for mistakes made in high school is preventing them from ever making up for those mistakes in college. What about a student who is sick or who has a disability? Do colleges account for those types of concerns in their process? Do they follow up with students with high GPAs who go on to do very poorly as college freshmen? This seems hypocritical. If low GPAs equal a risk, then shouldn't high GPAs be forced to prove that they can handle college and be successful as the admissions officer believed?

When a quality person is kept out of college simply because of a low GPA, everyone pays for that. That student could be missing out on a chance to do many people much good in the future. But we'll never know because someone decided that a 2.5 GPA in high school meant that the student was not "worthy" to attend their college. This is discrimination at its worst, only this type is completely accepted in today's society.

Again, we all pay when quality people are denied opportunity, even if they are people who have made mistakes at one time or another in high school. We are saying that in college, we lose compassion and forgiveness. Surely that's not what higher education is all about. Let's not put so much stake in a number. Get to know the applicant, and see in her eyes what she has the potential to do. That transcript is just a piece of paper. College should be about people, not paper.

Before we talk about the reason for the score, take a few minutes to list what you see that was done well in the piece:

_____

_____

_____

_____

_____

_____

_____

Here are some observations that I hope you made:

- was well-organized

- addressed the prompt and answered the question

- was tailored to an appropriate audience

- used persuasive language and examples

- used sentence variety and accurate/specific word choice

- was free of grammatical errors or other errors

Just to give you some comparative essays, here are a few other ranges: This would score a 1/6 on Writing Applications:

I don't think GPA should be used to let kids into college. Colleges should only look at what classes the student took and if they got a diploma.

You can see that this writer did provide an opinion, but it is simply not enough to get anywhere near answering the question.

This would score a 2/6 on Writing Applications:

> I think it is unfair to use GPA to decide college admissions. That number does tell you some things about a student, but there is much more to the story. For example, a student might go to a school that uses weighted grades. That way they may have had the same classes but have a higher GPA so it would be unfair.

In this case, the writer offers an opinion and begins to support it, but then he does not go on to develop his ideas.

When you complete the practice prompts for the OGT Reading and Writing tests that follow, compare what you wrote to the models that are provided here. Use that to note differences and areas where you can improve.

Pre-Game Talk:
Getting the Most Out of the Practice Tests

I'm sure you've taken hundreds of practice tests, but the ones you are about to take are designed not only to help you pass the Reading and Writing graduation tests but to score as high as you can—hopefully in the Accelerated and Advanced scoring ranges. Of course, much like sports, you will get out of them what you put in. If you use these practice tests as they are intended to be used, treat them as if they are the real thing, and look over the scoring explanations and sample responses, you will come away with the ability to do your best. Legendary coach John Wooden said, "Don't measure yourself by what you have accomplished, but what you should have accomplished with your ability." Look over the following reminders before you take your practice tests:

1. Follow directions. The tests are modeled very closely after the real tests, so if you can do it here, you can do it there.
2. Write on the test: mark up the directions, annotate the passages, cross out wrong choices, and do any other writing on the test that makes you more confident and comfortable.
3. Although they jokingly say "the best way to do well on a test is to know the right answers," don't forget the many strategies you have learned for multiple-choice tests: process of elimination, plugging in the right answer, and making an educated guess. Never leave a question blank.
4. If possible, put yourself in an environment like the one you'll have for the real test. You should also keep track of your time.
5. Try your best not to think this is just a practice test. That's the same as thinking that basketball practice is just practice. It's true, but in both cases if you treat it with less seriousness and attention, it's less effective.
6. At the same time, though, relax. Do your best and know that this will be a learning experience. This process is going to help you pass and score as high as you can on the Reading and Writing OGTs. This is simply the last hurdle.

PART 3

TWO PRACTICE OGT TESTS IN READING

Reading Practice
ANSWER SHEET—TEST 1

1 Ⓐ Ⓑ Ⓒ Ⓓ

2 Ⓐ Ⓑ Ⓒ Ⓓ

3 Ⓐ Ⓑ Ⓒ Ⓓ

4 Ⓐ Ⓑ Ⓒ Ⓓ

5 Write your response to question 5 in the space below.

6 Ⓐ Ⓑ Ⓒ Ⓓ

7 Ⓐ Ⓑ Ⓒ Ⓓ

Reading Practice
ANSWER SHEET—TEST 1

8 Write your response to question 8 in the space below.

_____

_____

_____

_____

_____

_____

_____

_____

_____

_____

_____

_____

_____

_____

9 Ⓐ Ⓑ Ⓒ Ⓓ

10 Ⓐ Ⓑ Ⓒ Ⓓ

11 Ⓐ Ⓑ Ⓒ Ⓓ

12 Ⓐ Ⓑ Ⓒ Ⓓ

13 Ⓐ Ⓑ Ⓒ Ⓓ

14 Ⓐ Ⓑ Ⓒ Ⓓ

Reading Practice
ANSWER SHEET—TEST 1

15 Write your response to question 15 in the space below.

---

16 Ⓐ Ⓑ Ⓒ Ⓓ

17 Ⓐ Ⓑ Ⓒ Ⓓ

18 Ⓐ Ⓑ Ⓒ Ⓓ

19 Ⓐ Ⓑ Ⓒ Ⓓ

20 Ⓐ Ⓑ Ⓒ Ⓓ

21 Ⓐ Ⓑ Ⓒ Ⓓ

22 Ⓐ Ⓑ Ⓒ Ⓓ

23 Ⓐ Ⓑ Ⓒ Ⓓ

Reading Practice
ANSWER SHEET—TEST 1

24 Ⓐ Ⓑ Ⓒ Ⓓ

25 Ⓐ Ⓑ Ⓒ Ⓓ

26 Write your response to question 26 in the space below.

27 Ⓐ Ⓑ Ⓒ Ⓓ

28 Ⓐ Ⓑ Ⓒ Ⓓ

Reading Practice

ANSWER SHEET—TEST 1

29 Write your response to question 29 in the space below.

30 Ⓐ Ⓑ Ⓒ Ⓓ

31 Ⓐ Ⓑ Ⓒ Ⓓ

32 Ⓐ Ⓑ Ⓒ Ⓓ

Reading Practice
ANSWER SHEET—TEST 1

33 Ⓐ Ⓑ Ⓒ Ⓓ

34 Ⓐ Ⓑ Ⓒ Ⓓ

Write your response to question 35 in the space below.

35

36 Ⓐ Ⓑ Ⓒ Ⓓ

Reading Practice
ANSWER SHEET—TEST 1

37 Write your response to question 37 in the space below.

38 Ⓐ Ⓑ Ⓒ Ⓓ

Reading Practice

ANSWER SHEET—TEST 1

39 Write your response to question 39 in the space below.

_____

_____

_____

_____

_____

_____

_____

_____

_____

_____

_____

_____

_____

_____

_____

_____

40 Ⓐ Ⓑ Ⓒ Ⓓ

41 Ⓐ Ⓑ Ⓒ Ⓓ

42 Ⓐ Ⓑ Ⓒ Ⓓ

43 Ⓐ Ⓑ Ⓒ Ⓓ

44 Ⓐ Ⓑ Ⓒ Ⓓ

Reading Practice

Reading Practice Test 1

Directions: Each passage in this test is followed by several questions. After reading the passage, choose the correct answer for each multiple-choice question, and then mark the corresponding circle in the Answer Document. If you change an answer, be sure to erase the first mark completely.

For the written-response questions, answer completely in the Answer Document in the space provided. You may not need to use the entire space provided.

You may refer to the passages as often as necessary. Make sure the number of the question in this test booklet corresponds to the number on the Answer Document. Be sure all your answers are complete and appear in the Answer Document.

Sixties Project

1   I had ADD before it was cool to have ADD. In fact, like <u>PTSD</u>,* ADD didn't even have a name, much less an acronym, when I joined the Marines and left for boot camp in January of 1967. It is possibly accurate to say that ADD was the insidious seed that ultimately blossomed into the PTSD that still tries to take my life from time to time. After four agonizing years in high school and two years in a junior college, I gave up on academics and enlisted. Football was the only thing I succeeded in during those four years, even though I tested extremely high on all of my aptitude tests, and I qualified as a semifinalist for the National Merit Scholarship test.

2   At Phoenix College, we won the national junior college championship in 1964. Then I got injured in the pre-season in my sophomore year, and everything fell apart. I couldn't play ball. I couldn't pass my classes. I needed another way to prove something to somebody or everybody. The Vietnam war was it.

---

*PTSD: Post-traumatic stress disorder is a psychiatric condition that can develop following any traumatic, catastropic life experience.

3   I got married to a wonderful girl three months after I met her in 1968. We were married for six months before I left with my squadron for Vietnam. Twenty-eight years later, we're still married. The word "miracle" is hopelessly inadequate. About three months before we left, I tried out for the Marine Corps football team and made it. After the coach, Major King Dixon, told me he was cutting orders to send me to Quantico, I respectfully declined. I wanted to go to Vietnam.

4   I was an avionics technician working on CH-46 helicopters. We arrived in-country on January 13, 1969. One night in February, my closest friend in the squadron, E. William "Billy Bump" Bolan told me that his wife just told him in her latest letter that she was pregnant. The next morning, he was killed by a sniper as his chopper left Marble Mountain with him on board as a machine-gunner. I never called or wrote to her. I went out on an occasional recovery mission during the next few months, prepping helicopters that had been shot down for extraction by CH-54 Sky Cranes.

5   In April, another one of our birds was shot down, killing all five people aboard. By this time, my fear combined with my belief that there was nothing there worth dying for to keep me from volunteering to fly as a machine-gunner as Billy had. I held out until August. I had to overcome the deep sense of cowardice that I was feeling by then, so I did it. The month went by without much happening. We flew a lot of re-supply missions, some medevacs, and some recon team inserts and extracts. Even though our pilots frequently told us that we should expect some heat on some of the missions, I never saw a muzzle flash. From time to time, we would find a few bullet holes in our plane after we landed, but that was it.

6   My last day of flying as a gunner was different. We had launched to fly re-supply, but we were immediately diverted to an emergency medevac on Barrier Island. Some Marines were pinned down, and had two serious casualties that needed emergency evacuation. We orbited while a Huey Cobra and an OV-10 Bronco came in to strafe the bad guys. The Cobra pilot put in a smoke rocket between the Marines and the enemy, The RTO on the ground gave the OV-10 pilot directions on where to attack. While we listened to the radio, we watched the OV-10 strafe on the wrong side of the smoke. We heard the RTO screaming for the pilot to "Check fire! You're killing friendlies!" while the pilot was shouting, "I've got them up and running! I'm going back in!" He finally realized what he had done, and flew away. We took out three KIAs and seven WIAs when we left. I wondered whether the Marines on the ground might shoot us when we landed to take on the casualties.

7   I spent most of my nights by myself at the Sergeants Club. As I looked out over the South China Sea, I saw a fiery explosion in the sky. The fireball fell into the sea, and then slowly spread, setting a small portion of the quiet horizon on fire. I heard the next day that a CH-53 had gone down in flames with four people on board. There was no known cause.

8   Christmas Eve, 1969. The base was shrouded in a dense fog that muffled sounds and strangled the spirit. Late in the afternoon, I was alone in my hootch, deep in melancholy. In three weeks, I would go home. I walked outside and sat down on the steps leading up to the door of the hootch. No

sounds. No movement. I felt as if I were in a sensory deprivation tank. Then I heard the seemingly distant sounds of a Huey helicopter. I looked up as the rotors got louder, and saw the helicopter pass low over my head at a speed only slightly faster than a hover. There was a red smoke grenade on one skid and a green one on the other. The Huey passed over me, and then pitched nose up until it looked like it would surely slide backwards and crash tail-first in front of me. But then the pilot kicked the rudder, and the nose and tail switched places. Then he went back over me and disappeared into the silence of the fog.

by Phil Carter

(http://www3.iath.virginia.edu/sixties/HTML_docs/Stories/Narratives/011story.html)

1. The author personifies the "dense fog that muffled sounds and strangled the spirit" in order to describe the

    A. oppression the soldiers felt in their surroundings.
    B. air because it was really hot in Vietnam.
    C. the smoke that was suffocating the soldiers.
    D. the way the soldiers felt about the glory of war.

2. To find out when the word "Huey" first entered the English language, you would look for which type of information in a dictionary?

    A. origin and etymology
    B. abbreviations used
    C. word derivatives
    D. variant pronunciations

3. The author suggests that his feelings of war

    A. changed when he discovered how much he missed his wife.
    B. stayed the same because he had always wanted to be a hero.
    C. changed when he realized nothing was worth dying for.
    D. stayed the same, he had lived war all of his life.

4. The author includes the scenario of the last time he flew as a gunner in order to show

    A. how the enemy can surprise any soldier with his tactics.
    B. that the enemies are people, too.
    C. the confusion that can take place in times of war.
    D. what happens to soldiers who disobey orders.

5. Explain what the author means when he says, "It is possibly accurate to say that ADD was the insidious seed that ultimately blossomed into the PTSD that still tries to take my life from time to time"; and give a detail or example from the passage to support your idea. Write your answer in the space provided on the Answer Sheet. (2 points)

6. Which most closely describes the author's reasons for writing this piece?

    A. He has Attention Deficit Disorder.
    B. He is unable to focus on one event at a time.
    C. There is no predictability in war.
    D. Sometimes war is necessary.

Video Games Numb Players To Violence

1   "It appears that individuals who play violent video games <u>habituate</u>, or 'get used to,' all the violence and eventually become physiologically numb to it," write Nicholas Carnagey, M.S., and colleagues.

2   "The modern entertainment media landscape could accurately be described as an effective systematic violence-desensitization tool," they add. Their article is in press for the Journal of Experimental Social Psychology. Carnagey is due to get a doctorate in psychology from Iowa State University this August. Carnagey's team studied 257 college students, 124 men and 133 women. First, the students noted their typical video game use. They also took aggression surveys and had their heart rate and galvanic skin response checked. (Galvanic skin response measures the skin's electrical resistance. It's an indication of bodily [physiological] arousal.)

3   Next, the students played either a violent or nonviolent video game for 20 minutes. The violent video games were Carmageddon, Duke Nukem, Mortal Kombat, and Future Cop. The nonviolent video games were Glider Pro, 3D Pinball, 3D Munch Man, and Tetra Madness. When the game session ended, the students repeated the heart rate and galvanic skin response tests. Both groups showed similar results. But the study wasn't over yet.

4   The students' last task: Watch a 10-minute videotape of real-life violence (shootings, prison fights, police confrontations, and courtroom outbursts). During the screening, the researchers monitored the students' heart rate and galvanic skin responses. Students who had played violent video games showed less <u>physiological response</u> to the real-life videos. The study "demonstrates that violent video game exposure can cause desensitization to real-life violence," write Carnagey and colleagues. "Children receive high doses of media violence," they note. "It initially is packaged in ways that are not too threatening, with cute cartoon-like characters," the researchers continue. "Older children consume increasingly threatening and realistic violence, but the increases are gradual and always in a way that is fun." Which medium is most desensitizing: TV, movies, or video games? And are some people more affected than others? Those are good questions for future research, Carnagey's team notes.

Carnagey, N. Journal of Experimental Social Psychology, July 17, 2006; online edition.
(**http://www.cbsnews.com/stories/2006/07/31/health/webmd/main1849262.shtm**)

7. Which technique does the author use to have readers view the information presented in the article as credible?

   A. The author makes it clear that she is discussing two research articles.
   B. The author details the experiment performed.
   C. The author expresses surprise at the amount of violence it took to make the study accurate.
   D. The author struggles with expressing difficult material into her own words.

8. The author uses many psychological terms in this article. Which definition means the same as <u>physiological response</u>?

   A. response in sweat
   B. bodily response
   C. visual response
   D. electrical current response.

9. Which statement represents the main idea of the article?

   A. Video game violence is bad.
   B. Research shows there is a connection between violent video game playing and a less-shocked response from that same person when watching real violence on television.
   C. Physiology is a fascinating topic of study because it shows that people sweat a lot while watching video games that are violent.
   D. There are no physiological connections between violent video game playing and a reaction to violence on television.

10. Describe a picture or other graphic that would help a reader more clearly understand or be more interested in the ideas of the passage. Give two specific examples from the passage that support your choice of a picture or a graphic. Write your answer in the space provided on the Answer Sheet. (2 points)

11. How do psychologists know that violent video game usage affects the body physiologically?

    A. They read a lot of research to support their claims.
    B. They have discovered that men were more violent if they played violent video games.
    C. They have discovered through a study of monkeys that those that played violent video games became more numb to violence on television.
    D. They have discovered, through a study of both men and women, that those who had played violent video games became more numb to the violence they witnessed on television.

12. How does the author surprise the reader in this passage?

   A. The reader does not expect the author to say, "But the study wasn't over yet," as there were already findings mentioned.
   B. The reader does not expect the author to report that the violence in video games affected men and women when watching television.
   C. The reader does not expect the author to state that physiological responses were measured.
   D. The reader expects the author to be one of the scientists.

13. What was the evidence presented in the article of "the modern entertainment media landscape could accurately be described as an effective systematic violence-desensitization tool"?

   A. The students played 20 minutes of violent video games.
   B. Students who had played violent video games showed less physiological response to the real-life videos.
   C. Students receive high dosages of violence in the media.
   D. The violent video games were Carmageddon, Duke Nukem, Mortal Kombat, and Future Cop. The nonviolent video games were Glider Pro, 3D Pinball, 3D Munch Man, and Tetra Madness.

14. What evidence does the author present for the idea that it is unclear as to what is more desensitizing, video games or violence in the media?

   A. "It initially is packaged in ways that are not too threatening, with cute cartoon-like characters," the researchers continue. "Older children consume increasingly threatening and realistic violence, but the increases are gradual and always in a way that is fun."
   B. "Children receive high doses of media violence," they note.
   C. "Which medium is most desensitizing: TV, movies, or video games? And are some people more affected than others?"
   D. Students who had played violent video games showed less physiological response to the real-life videos.

15. Which definition means the same as <u>habituate</u> does in this sentence from paragraph 1: "It appears that individuals who play violent video games habituate, or 'get used to,' all the violence and eventually become physiologically numb to it . . . ."?

   A. to repeat a function in excess
   B. to destroy a particular brain function
   C. to record a particular situation
   D. to become accustomed to a particular situation

An Apology to the Graduates

You all will live longer than any generation in history, yet you were kicked into high gear earlier as well. How exhausted you must be.

By Anna Quindlen *Newsweek* May 17 issue

1   Members of the class of 2004:
I'm so sorry.
I look at all of you and realize that, for many, life has been a relentless treadmill since you entered preschool at the age of 2. Sometimes, as though I am narrating a fairy story, I tell my children of a time when the SAT was taken only once and a tutor was a character in an English novel, when I could manage to pay my own college tuition with summer wages and find both a good job and a decent apartment when I graduated.

2   Now cottage industries have grown up around the impossibility of any of that: specialized learning centers to supplement schools, special loan programs at <u>usurious</u> rates to supplement college grants, companies that will throw up instant walls to turn a one-bedroom apartment into a place where three people can coexist.

3   There's an honorable tradition of starving students; it's just that, between the outsourcing of jobs and a boom market in real estate, your generation envisions becoming starving adults. Caught in our peculiar modern nexus of prosperity and insolvency, easy credit and epidemic bankruptcy, you also get toxic messages from the culture about what achievement means. It is no longer enough to make it; you must make it BIG. Television has turned everything into a contest, from courtship to adoption. In a voyeuristic world, fame becomes a ubiquitous career goal.

4   You all will live longer than any generation in history, yet you were kicked into high gear earlier as well. How exhausted you must be. Your college applications look like the resumes for midlevel executives. We boomer moms and dads had high expectations, ratcheted up by what the more honest of us must admit was something akin to competitive parenting. Soccer leagues. Language programs. Even summer camps that concentrate on college prep instead of sailing. Your grandparents surely think that it was more stressful to join the service after Pearl Harbor, and at some level they're right. But the mission was clear then, the goal straightforward and honorable, the endgame a good life and a healthy family. What is it now? Public buildings were once named after war heroes, philanthropists and presidents, but in New Jersey one school has managed to keep its gym spiffy by taking money from the local supermarket and putting up a big sign: THE SHOPRITE OF BROOKLAWN CENTER. Cash is the point. Who wants to be a millionaire? Everyone. Although a million doesn't buy what it once did. Just look at the bottom line on your college loans.

5   Who can blame you if you were not all creating Campus Coalition's for Peace or People for the Ethical Treatment of People? It was not marches or leafleting that drove the political process as you grew up, but soft money and PACs. It now costs so much to run a race for public office that the contribution of any individual may seem puny and irrelevant. Your commencements will take place in the shadow of the revelation that some American

troops, styled as heroic liberators, were instead sadistic humiliators in the prisons of Iraq. You new women have a new anti-role model, the G.I. Jane photographed pointing at the genitals of the naked Iraqi and smirking.

6 One professor at the University of Maryland, who was at the college during the '60s and remembers thousands gathering to protest the Vietnam War, told the Baltimore Sun the activist days are gone forever: "They're interested in their grades and then getting a good job when they get out." It's easy to translate this transformation into vacuous careerism, but it's something more complex than that. Here is a remarkably incisive summation from Lillian Mongeau, who will graduate from Barnard College later this month:

"When telling my family history I proudly tell how each generation sacrificed so that the next could achieve more—more education, more money, more prestige. But how can I achieve more than my parents? They are living the American dream. Now if I don't achieve as much as they did I will have failed, but to achieve more than they did is virtually impossible. To this is the added pressure that there is no excuse for failure. I have had the best of everything . . . if I mess up it will be entirely my fault." "I feel that I just need some time," she adds. "I just want everything to stop moving for a while so that I can think."

7 To the members of the class of 2004: putting a stop to this treadmill is like disarmament. Who dares to go first? A generation ago your parents, as a group, were known for wanting to give peace a chance in the world. Somehow we have raised a group that wants only a little peace in their own frantic lives. But peace is not what you see in the immediate future, for the world, for this nation or for yourselves. Instead, what stretches before you looks like a version of "Survivor" in street clothes. Find the job. Find the mate. Scale the ladder. Have the baby. Make the deal. Make the birthday cake. The gym, the Gap, the lover, the decor, the cuisine. Who will win the contest? Perhaps it will be those of you brave enough to stop moving.

16. The author compares the graduating class' life to being one that is done on an endless treadmill. Why is that?

A. A treadmill is a conveyor belt that continues until shut off.
B. A treadmill is a something that a student could control by turning the switch on or off.
C. A treadmill goes slowly, so it is an easy way to keep up the pace.
D. A treadmill goes too quickly for anyone to keep up.

17. "Now cottage industries have grown up around the impossibility of any of that: specialized learning centers to supplement schools, special loan programs at usurious rates to supplement college grants, companies that will throw up instant walls to turn a one-bedroom apartment into a place where three people can coexist."

Which word represents the meaning of <u>usurious</u>?

A. boring
B. thorough
C. small
D. outrageous

18. What is the purpose of the sentence after the title, "You all will live longer than any generation in history, yet you were kicked into high gear earlier as well. How exhausted you must be"?

A. to convince the reader that being a kid is exhausting
B. to introduce the essay and set the tone
C. to clarify a reference made later in the essay
D. to show what life is like

19. Summarize paragraph 4. Write your answer in the space provided on the Answer Sheet. (2 points)

20. The author says compared with the Vietnam generation

A. the young generation would like to give peace a chance and protest the Iraqi war.
B. the young generation is more interested in their own personal success.
C. the young generation would like a piece of the millions they must achieve.
D. the young generation would like to protest trying to earn millions of dollars because it isn't possible.

21. According to the author, an opportunity for a good life will be possible if

A. the members of the graduating class get a job, get married, have a baby, go to the gym, and make a lot of money.
B. the members of the graduating class get on treadmills and start working out.
C. the members of the graduating class stop moving.
D. the members of the graduating class drop out of college.

Exclusive results: Teens & Celebrities

Teen People's managing editor, Lori Majewski, shares her unique perspective as we explore the surprising responses American teens gave on the subject of fame and fortune.

1   When I was a teenager growing up in New Jersey in the 1980s, my girl-friends and I were obsessed with Duran Duran. We went to see their concerts, swooned over their videos on MTV, and snatched up every album, 45 and 12-inch remix we could find (yes, this was in the days of vinyl and cassettes). Although our goal was to someday meet any or all of the band members, we never thought we would get closer to them and their fabulous VIP lives than the posters on our walls. The same went for other friends who adored Rob Lowe and the Coreys (Haim and Feldman). These celebrities may as well have lived on another planet. One could argue that the relationship between teens and celebrities had remained relatively unchanged from the Elvis Presley mania of the mid-1950s to the boy-band craze of the late '90s. However, as managing editor of "Teen People," I have learned that this generation of teenagers is not satisfied with merely staring at posters or even rubbing shoulders with their favorite stars—they want to be them. And in their minds, it is far from an impossible dream.

2   Consider the <u>currency</u> of the many celebrity weeklies and websites: showing boldfaced names doing banal things like taking the garbage to the curb, talking on their cellphones or making the ever-popular Starbucks run. Today's kids constantly see stars being just like the rest of us, so it's little wonder they believe they can be just like them.

3   Furthering this <u>notion</u>? Reality TV. Teens know that at any minute, MTV might come to their town and turn them and their friends into the next big things, just like it did with the young stars of the California-based "Laguna Beach: The Real Orange County." The real-life soap is so popular that one of its main players, Lauren "LC" Conrad, 20, scored her own spinoff, "The Hills;" meanwhile, her Laguna nemesis, Kristin Cavallari, 19, is being offered movie roles. The more proactive star wannabes don't wait for fame to come to them. They try out for TV talent shows like "American Idol." Hey, even if they can't carry a tune, they can make a spectacle of themselves during the audition and score big money, like "Idol's" William Hung. Teens who don't want to subject themselves to Simon Cowell have found other paths to stardom. Teens aspire to be like stars, but they don't necessarily view them as role models. Using her webcam to capture herself and another girl singing the Backstreet Boys' "Get Down," one girl recently received more than 152,000 hits with her cute but unremarkable clip.

4   Because so many teens see themselves as stars, it's no wonder they have a different relationship with bona fide celebrities than any previous generation. USA WEEKEND Magazine's Teens & Celebrities survey reveals that although more than a third (36%) believe talent is more important than personality in a celebrity, only slightly fewer teens (32%) said personality outranks talent. So of course teens think they have a decent shot at stardom when they don't think it requires them to be a singer or actor of extraordinary skill. The survey also finds that teens want to look and act like famous people, and although that has been true through the ages, they're taking more drastic steps

to do so. About 60% think teens want to pierce a body part or get a tattoo because a celebrity has. Roughly half agree that their own peers drink or smoke cigarettes because they see their idols doing it. And 77% believe that when a star loses weight, teenagers are prone do the same—although only 13% admit to having gone on a diet to look more like a celebrity.

5   There's a paradox in these survey results: Teens aspire to be like stars, but they don't necessarily view them as role models. When it comes to issues such as war and politics, celebrities rank dead last on the list of people teens say influence their opinions, behind parents, friends, teachers and the media. That's why they tend to tune out most stars who talk about environmental issues and world peace. According to the survey, 78% of teens say they don't think more about charitable causes when celebrities participate in fundraisers, and more than half (52%) suspect that stars use charity events for self-promotion.

6   These stats don't mean we're raising a generation of skeptics—just smart kids. Dubbed by USA WEEKEND as "Generation Give" last year, today's teens are able to distinguish a passionate star from one who's just looking for good press. There are true celebrity humanitarians, like Angelina Jolie, who demonstrates her commitment to developing nations. Seeing her practice what she preaches makes teenagers, many of whom call her an inspiration, put even more energy into doing good works. Indeed, in last year's Teens & Volunteering survey, 96% of teens say they volunteer.

7   Every year, "Teen People's" April issue features "20 Teens Who Will Change the World." And every year, we find that the scope of what these teens are doing—and where they're doing it—broadens. In 2006, we found teens who volunteered in locales like Sri Lanka, Guinea and Peru. At our luncheon honoring these kids, celebrity host Nick Lachey called them an inspiration and was just as excited to meet these do-gooders as they were to meet him. It makes you wonder: Maybe by the time the next generation of teens comes around, the stars will be striving to be just like them.

(http://www.usaweekend.com/06_issues/060521/060521teens_and_celebs.html)

22.   The author suggests

    A.   teens haven't changed much over the years.
    B.   teens are losing a sense of reality.
    C.   teens admire stars.
    D.   teens want to be the stars they admire.

23.   Using the information in the passage as a guide, define the word <u>currency</u>. Give a context clue from the passage that helped you come to your definition. Write your answer in the space provided on the Answer Sheet. (2 points)

24. Which quotation supports the author's view that teens are considered "Generation Give"?

    A. "Teens aspire to be like stars, but they don't necessarily view them as role models."
    B. "Teens aspire to be like stars, but they don't necessarily view them as stars."
    C. "In 2006, we found teens who volunteered in locales like Sri Lanka, Guinea and Peru."
    D. "The survey also finds that teens want to look and act like famous people, and although that has been true through the ages, they're taking more drastic steps to do so."

25. Which definition most closely means <u>notion</u> as used in the quotation, "Furthering this notion"?

    A. falsehood
    B. idea
    C. lie
    D. persuasion

26. According to the information given in the article, the author feels that

    A. the teens of the future have a good chance of impacting Hollywood for the better.
    B. the teens of the future are doomed for a lot of disappointment.
    C. the teens of the future will be conquering Hollywood with their talents.
    D. the teens of the future will be unsure what talent truly is.

27. This passage is about

    A. teenagers having eating disorders because of their Hollywood role models.
    B. teenagers having trouble volunteering because many people in Hollywood are not humanitarians.
    C. the possibility that some teenagers are looking for instant popularity while others have a clear sense that volunteering is more rewarding.
    D. Angelina Jolie as a great role model because of her humanitarianism.

28. "When it comes to issues such as war and politics, celebrities rank dead last on the list of people teens say influence their opinions, behind parents, friends, teachers and the media."

    This sentence from paragraph 5 can be paraphrased as:

    A. Celebrities rank dead last on the list of people teens say influence their opinions, behind parents, friends, teachers, and others.
    B. Issues such as war and politics are ranked poorly by teens behind parents, friends, teachers, and the media.
    C. Celebrity opinions do not rank as highly as parents, friends, teachers, and the media when it comes to topics such as war and politics.
    D. Teachers, media, parents, and friends rate higher than war and politics behind the celebrities.

29. Explain how the author views celebrities as role models. Support your explanation by giving three examples or details from the passage. Write your answer in the **Answer Document**. (4 points)

30. The author includes survey results (paragraph 4) in order to show

    A. that a majority of teenagers believe celebrities are role models.
    B. that a majority of teenagers model their images after celebrities.
    C. that a majority of celebrities are trying to be more like the teenagers of the future.
    D. that a majority of celebrities change their image in order to influence teenagers.

The Bet

Note: This is a challenging and somewhat lengthy short story, but the reading passages on the OGT are likely to become more challenging each year, so this will be excellent practice for you.

1   IT WAS a dark autumn night. The old banker was walking up and down his study and remembering how, fifteen years before, he had given a party one autumn evening. There had been many clever men there, and there had been interesting conversations. Among other things they had talked of capital punishment. The majority of the guests, among whom were many journalists and intellectual men, disapproved of the death penalty. They considered that form of punishment out of date, immoral, and unsuitable for Christian States. In the opinion of some of them the death penalty ought to be replaced everywhere by imprisonment for life. "I don't agree with you," said their host the banker. "I have not tried either the death penalty or imprisonment for life, but if one may judge <u>a priori</u>,* the death penalty is more moral and more humane than imprisonment for life. Capital punishment kills a man at once, but lifelong imprisonment kills him slowly. Which executioner is the more humane, he who kills you in a few minutes or he who drags the life out of you in the course of many years?"

2   "Both are equally immoral," observed one of the guests, "for they both have the same object—to take away life. The State is not God. It has not the right to take away what it cannot restore when it wants to." Among the guests was a young lawyer, a young man of five-and-twenty. When he was asked his opinion, he said: "The death sentence and the life sentence are equally immoral, but if I had to choose between the death penalty and imprisonment for life, I would certainly choose the second. To live anyhow is better than not at all." A lively discussion arose. The banker, who was younger and more nervous in those days, was suddenly carried away by excitement; he struck the table with his fist and shouted at the young man: "It's not true! I'll bet you two millions you wouldn't stay in solitary confinement for five years."

---

*<u>a priori</u>: Latin for "the former."

3 "If you mean that in earnest," said the young man, "I'll take the bet, but I would stay not five but fifteen years."

"Fifteen? Done!" cried the banker. "Gentlemen, I stake two millions!"

"Agreed! You stake your millions and I stake my freedom!" said the young man.

And this wild, senseless bet was carried out! The banker, spoilt and frivolous, with millions beyond his reckoning, was delighted at the bet. At supper he made fun of the young man, and said:

"Think better of it, young man, while there is still time. To me two millions are a trifle, but you are losing three or four of the best years of your life. I say three or four, because you won't stay longer. Don't forget either, you unhappy man, that voluntary confinement is a great deal harder to bear than compulsory. The thought that you have the right to step out in liberty at any moment will poison your whole existence in prison. I am sorry for you."

4 And now the banker, walking to and fro, remembered all this, and asked himself: "What was the object of that bet? What is the good of that man's losing fifteen years of his life and my throwing away two millions? Can it prove that the death penalty is better or worse than imprisonment for life? No, no. It was all nonsensical and meaningless. On my part it was the <u>caprice</u>* of a pampered man, and on his part simple greed for money. . . ."

5 Then he remembered what followed that evening. It was decided that the young man should spend the years of his captivity under the strictest supervision in one of the lodges in the banker's garden. It was agreed that for fifteen years he should not be free to cross the threshold of the lodge, to see human beings, to hear the human voice, or to receive letters and newspapers. He was allowed to have a musical instrument and books, and was allowed to write letters, to drink wine, and to smoke. By the terms of the agreement, the only relations he could have with the outer world were by a little window made purposely for that object. He might have anything he wanted—books, music, wine, and so on—in any quantity he desired by writing an order, but could only receive them through the window. The agreement provided for every detail and every trifle that would make his imprisonment strictly solitary, and bound the young man to stay there exactly fifteen years, beginning from twelve o'clock of November 14, 1870, and ending at twelve o'clock of November 14, 1885. The slightest attempt on his part to break the conditions, if only two minutes before the end, released the banker from the obligation to pay him two millions.

6 For the first year of his confinement, as far as one could judge from his brief notes, the prisoner suffered severely from loneliness and depression. The sounds of the piano could be heard continually day and night from his lodge. He refused wine and tobacco. Wine, he wrote, excites the desires, and desires are the worst foes of the prisoner; and besides, nothing could be more dreary than drinking good wine and seeing no one. And tobacco spoilt the air of his room. In the first year the books he sent for were principally of a light character; novels with a complicated love plot, sensational

*<u>Caprice</u>: sudden idea.

and fantastic stories, and so on. In the second year the piano was silent in the lodge, and the prisoner asked only for the classics. In the fifth year music was audible again, and the prisoner asked for wine. Those who watched him through the window said that all that year he spent doing nothing but eating and drinking and lying on his bed, frequently yawning and angrily talking to himself. He did not read books. Sometimes at night he would sit down to write; he would spend hours writing, and in the morning tear up all that he had written. More than once he could be heard crying. In the second half of the sixth year the prisoner began zealously studying languages, philosophy, and history. He threw himself eagerly into these studies—so much so that the banker had enough to do to get him the books he ordered. In the course of four years some six hundred volumes were procured at his request. It was during this period that the banker received the following letter from his prisoner:

7   "My dear Jailer, I write you these lines in six languages. Show them to people who know the languages. Let them read them. If they find not one mistake I implore you to fire a shot in the garden. That shot will show me that my efforts have not been thrown away. The geniuses of all ages and of all lands speak different languages, but the same flame burns in them all. Oh, if you only knew what unearthly happiness my soul feels now from being able to understand them!" The prisoner's desire was fulfilled. The banker ordered two shots to be fired in the garden.

8   Then after the tenth year, the prisoner sat immovably at the table and read nothing but the Gospel. It seemed strange to the banker that a man who in four years had mastered six hundred learned volumes should waste nearly a year over one thin book easy of comprehension. Theology and histories of religion followed the Gospels.

9   In the last two years of his confinement the prisoner read an immense quantity of books quite <u>indiscriminately</u>. At one time he was busy with the natural sciences, then he would ask for Byron or Shakespeare. There were notes in which he demanded at the same time books on chemistry, and a manual of medicine, and a novel, and some treatise on philosophy or theology. His reading suggested a man swimming in the sea among the wreckage of his ship, and trying to save his life by greedily clutching first at one spar and then at another.

10   The old banker remembered all this, and thought:
"To-morrow at twelve o'clock he will regain his freedom. By our agreement I ought to pay him two millions. If I do pay him, it is all over with me: I shall be utterly ruined."

11   Fifteen years before, his millions had been beyond his reckoning; now he was afraid to ask himself which were greater, his debts or his assets. Desperate gambling on the Stock Exchange, wild speculation and the excitability which he could not get over even in advancing years, had by degrees led to the decline of his fortune and the proud, fearless, self-confident millionaire had become a banker of middling rank, trembling at every rise and fall in his investments. "Cursed bet!" muttered the old man, clutching his head in despair "Why didn't the man die? He is only forty now. He will take my last penny from me, he will marry, will enjoy life, will gamble

on the Exchange; while I shall look at him with envy like a beggar, and hear from him every day the same sentence: 'I am indebted to you for the happiness of my life, let me help you!' No, it is too much! The one means of being saved from bankruptcy and disgrace is the death of that man!" It struck three o'clock, the banker listened; everyone was asleep in the house and nothing could be heard outside but the rustling of the chilled trees. Trying to make no noise, he took from a fireproof safe the key of the door which had not been opened for fifteen years, put on his overcoat, and went out of the house. It was dark and cold in the garden. Rain was falling. A damp cutting wind was racing about the garden, howling and giving the trees no rest. The banker strained his eyes, but could see neither the earth nor the white statues, nor the lodge, nor the trees. Going to the spot where the lodge stood, he twice called the watchman. No answer followed. Evidently the watchman had sought shelter from the weather, and was now asleep somewhere either in the kitchen or in the greenhouse.

12 "If I had the <u>pluck</u>* to carry out my intention," thought the old man, "suspicion would fall first upon the watchman."

13 He felt in the darkness for the steps and the door, and went into the entry of the lodge. Then he groped his way into a little passage and lighted a match. There was not a soul there. There was a bedstead with no bedding on it, and in the corner there was a dark cast-iron stove. The seals on the door leading to the prisoner's rooms were intact.

14 When the match went out the old man, trembling with emotion, peeped through the little window. A candle was burning dimly in the prisoner's room. He was sitting at the table. Nothing could be seen but his back, the hair on his head, and his hands. Open books were lying on the table, on the two easy-chairs, and on the carpet near the table.

15 Five minutes passed and the prisoner did not once stir. Fifteen years' imprisonment had taught him to sit still. The banker tapped at the window with his finger, and the prisoner made no movement whatever in response. Then the banker cautiously broke the seals off the door and put the key in the keyhole. The rusty lock gave a grating sound and the door creaked. The banker expected to hear at once footsteps and a cry of astonishment, but three minutes passed and it was as quiet as ever in the room. He made up his mind to go in. At the table a man unlike ordinary people was sitting motionless. He was a skeleton with the skin drawn tight over his bones, with long curls like a woman's and a shaggy beard. His face was yellow with an earthy tint in it, his cheeks were hollow, his back long and narrow, and the hand on which his shaggy head was propped was so thin and delicate that it was dreadful to look at it. His hair was already streaked with silver, and seeing his emaciated, aged-looking face, no one would have believed that he was only forty. He was asleep. . . . In front of his bowed head there lay on the table a sheet of paper on which there was something written in fine handwriting.

---

*<u>Pluck</u>: courage.

16 "Poor creature!" thought the banker, "he is asleep and most likely dreaming of the millions. And I have only to take this half-dead man, throw him on the bed, stifle him a little with the pillow, and the most conscientious expert would find no sign of a violent death. But let us first read what he has written here. . . ."
The banker took the page from the table and read as follows:
"To-morrow at twelve o'clock I regain my freedom and the right to associate with other men, but before I leave this room and see the sunshine, I think it necessary to say a few words to you. With a clear conscience I tell you, as before God, who beholds me, that I despise freedom and life and health, and all that in your books is called the good things of the world.

17 "For fifteen years I have been intently studying earthly life. It is true I have not seen the earth nor men, but in your books I have drunk fragrant wine, I have sung songs, I have hunted stags and wild boars in the forests, have loved women. . . . Beauties as ethereal as clouds, created by the magic of your poets and geniuses, have visited me at night, and have whispered in my ears wonderful tales that have set my brain in a whirl. In your books I have climbed to the peaks of Elburz and Mont Blanc, and from there I have seen the sun rise and have watched it at evening flood the sky, the ocean, and the mountain-tops with gold and crimson. I have watched from there the lightning flashing over my head and cleaving the storm-clouds. I have seen green forests, fields, rivers, lakes, towns. I have heard the singing of the sirens, and the strains of the shepherds' pipes; I have touched the wings of comely devils who flew down to converse with me of God. . . . In your books I have flung myself into the bottomless pit, performed miracles, slain, burned towns, preached new religions, conquered whole kingdoms. . . ."Your books have given me wisdom. All that the unresting thought of man has created in the ages is compressed into a small compass in my brain. I know that I am wiser than all of you.

18 "And I despise your books, I despise wisdom and the blessings of this world. It is all worthless, fleeting, illusory, and deceptive, like a mirage. You may be proud, wise, and fine, but death will wipe you off the face of the earth as though you were no more than mice burrowing under the floor, and your posterity, your history, your immortal geniuses will burn or freeze together with the earthly globe. "You have lost your reason and taken the wrong path. You have taken lies for truth, and hideousness for beauty. You would marvel if, owing to strange events of some sorts, frogs and lizards suddenly grew on apple and orange trees instead of fruit, or if roses began to smell like a sweating horse; so I marvel at you who exchange heaven for earth. I don't want to understand you.

19 "To prove to you in action how I despise all that you live by, I renounce the two millions of which I once dreamed as of paradise and which now I despise. To deprive myself of the right to the money I shall go out from here five hours before the time fixed, and so break the compact. . . ."

20 When the banker had read this he laid the page on the table, kissed the strange man on the head, and went out of the lodge, weeping. At no other time, even when he had lost heavily on the Stock Exchange, had he felt so

great a contempt for himself. When he got home he lay on his bed, but his tears and emotion kept him for hours from sleeping.

21 Next morning the watchmen ran in with pale faces, and told him they had seen the man who lived in the lodge climb out of the window into the garden, go to the gate, and disappear. The banker went at once with the servants to the lodge and made sure of the flight of his prisoner. To avoid arousing unnecessary talk, he took from the table the writing in which the millions were renounced, and when he got home locked it up in the fireproof safe.

by Anton Chekhov

31. Which of the excerpts illustrates the banker's contempt for himself?

   A. "To avoid arousing unnecessary talk, he took from the table the writing in which the millions were renounced, and when he got home locked it up in the fireproof safe."
   B. "And I despise your books, I despise wisdom and the blessings of this world. It is all worthless, fleeting, illusory, and deceptive, like a mirage."
   C. "He was a skeleton with the skin drawn tight over his bones, with long curls like a woman's and a shaggy beard."
   D. "His reading suggested a man swimming in the sea among the wreckage of his ship, and trying to save his life by greedily clutching first at one spar and then at another."

32. Why did the lawyer give up the money?

   A. He felt money was the reason he wasted his life.
   B. He learned how to make more money through the books he read.
   C. He was going insane because he read so many books.
   D. The books he read showed him how money caused the banker to be greedy.

33. Which word best describes the tone of the last paragraph?

   A. relief
   B. guilt
   C. failure
   D. disbelief

34. Which of the statements below describes a theme from the short story?

   A. Wealth can be measured in more than monetary value.
   B. Money makes men crazy.
   C. People will do anything for money.
   D. Imprisonment makes people too well educated.

35. Explain how the concept of irony is used throughout the story. Use three details or examples from the story to support your answer. Write your answer in the space provided on the Answer Sheet. (4 points)

36. What was the author's purpose in telling the reader that the banker enclosed the letter in a safe?

    A. The letter proved that the banker had won the bet.
    B. The lawyer learned nothing while imprisoned.
    C. The banker killed the lawyer and hid his body.
    D. It shows the reader that not much has changed despite the experiment.

37. Based on the information provided in paragraph 9, <u>indiscriminately</u> means

    A. quickly making a decision.
    B. lovingly, completed with much care.
    C. lacking in care, judgment, selectivity.
    D. thoughtfully.

38. In paragraph 15 how does the image of the lawyer contribute to the theme of the short story?

    A. His hunched-over appearance suggests that he is losing his mind.
    B. His thin figure helps to show that he does not feel he needs much of what the outside world has to offer. He is able to live on the bare minimum.
    C. His hunched-over appearance suggests that he is ready to have a feast when he is released. He cannot wait to spend the money on a large banquet of food.
    D. His thin figure helps to show that he is conserving his energy for his release.

39. Explain how the narrator emphasizes the lack of understanding that the banker has in regard to wealth. Use information from the story to support your answer. Write your response in the space provided on the Answer Sheet. (4 points)

Part I: Life

1   Success is counted sweetest
     By those who ne'er succeed.
     To comprehend a nectar
     Requires sorest need.

2   Not one of all the purple host
     Who took the flag to-day
     Can tell the definition,
     So clear, of victory!

3   As he, defeated, dying,
     On whose forbidden ear
     The distant strains of triumph
     Burst agonized and clear!

     By Emily Dickinson

40. Based on the information in lines 1–4 of the poem, which sentence gives the best interpretation of that passage?

  A. Those who have never experienced a struggle cannot understand success.
  B. Those who long for success never can achieve success.
  C. Those who would work hard for success can obtain it with ease.
  D. Those who are in battle can obtain victory.

41. Which best represents the theme of the poem?

  A. Success often comes with money.
  B. Success often comes after the person has sacrificed for it.
  C. Success often comes if one feels successful.
  D. Success often comes with victory on the battlefield.

42. In the last stanza of the poem, the author says: "As he, defeated, dying, / On whose forbidden ear / The distant strains of / triumph / Burst, agonized and clear."

  Which sentence below represents her intended meaning?

  A. Triumph is clear to those who have felt success.
  B. Triumph is clear to those who want it to be.
  C. Triumph is clear to those who have nearly died for their success.
  D. Triumph is only clear to soldiers.

43. In lines 5–8, when the author refers to "who took the flag today," what point is she making?

  A. He who gains the flag is victorious.
  B. He who gains the flag is an American.
  C. He who gains a Purple Heart gets an American flag.
  D. He who gains an American flag gets a Purple Heart.

44. The poet's purpose is most likely to

  A. describe a famous soldier who was victorious.
  B. pay tribute to the fallen soldiers lost at sea.
  C. show that victory does not come without cost.
  D. depict victory as being a savage animal.

If there is still time remaining, you may review your answers.

Reading Practice
ANSWER KEY—TEST 1

1. A
2. A
3. C
4. C
5. See Answers and Explanations
6. C
7. B
8. B
9. B
10. See Answers and Explanations
11. D
12. A
13. B
14. C
15. D

16. A
17. D
18. B
19. See Answers and Explanations
20. B
21. C
22. D
23. See Answers and Explanations
24. C
25. B
26. A
27. C
28. C
29. See Answers and Explanations
30. B

31. A
32. D
33. B
34. A
35. See Answers and Explanations
36. D
37. C
38. B
39. See Answers and Explanations
40. A
41. B
42. C
43. A
44. C

ANSWERS AND EXPLANATIONS

Reading Practice

1. **(A)** oppression the soldiers felt in their surroundings.

   This matches the overall feel of the piece. Also, B seems too simplistic, and D mentions "glory of war," which seems not to fit.

2. **(A)** origin and etymology

   Choices B and D do not match the task of finding out when a word entered the language. Though the word *derivative* means that you would get some information about this, "origin and etymology" is the exact right answer.

3. **(C)** changed when he realized nothing was worth dying for.

   Considering how the writer describes his feelings in the beginning, B and D do not seem logical answers. His wife is only mentioned in paragraph 3, so that excludes A as the better answer. Paragraph 5, where the idea in choice C appears, seems to indicate a turning point.

4. **(C)** the confusion that can take place in times of war.

   Choices B and D do not fit very well. They seem too much like themes, and this question is not asking about that. A is perhaps a true statement, but considering the author's description of the events, C is the best fit.

5. This question clearly asks for two separate pieces of information. Sample answer:

   1. The author means that having ADD caused him to go through the ordeal that led to PTSD.
   2. The author goes on to talk about joining the war because he was not successful in school, probably because of having ADD.

6. **(C)** There is no predictability in war.

   A is a trick because ADD is mentioned and will look familiar. D does not seem at all what the author is trying to say. B does not seem like it fits, because the author clearly can focus on one event. C fits well, because the author feels that everything changed and was not what he imagined in the beginning.

7. **(B)** The author details the experiment performed.

   Since *credible* means "believable," the correct answer must be something that a reader would find logical. Options C and D are not likely to make you feel the writer is believable. A is useful information, but details about the actual experiment (Choice B) are certainly what is expected of any quality study.

8. **(B)** bodily response

   This is a vocabulary-in-context question. You can look at roots, suffixes, prefixes, and certainly go back and look at how the word is used in the piece. The term is used in paragraph 2 and in paragraph 4 after mention of heart rate and skin response. This makes B a better choice than A, since A only mentions "sweat."

9. **(B)** Research shows there is a connection between violent video game playing and a less-shocked response from that same person when watching real violence on television.

   Choice A is far too simplistic. It's unlikely a research study would jump to that conclusion. D is simply incorrect. C starts off nice but then focuses on watching people sweat, which is not the focus of the overall study and article.

10. For this, you have to name a graphic. In an article like this, reasonable choices are graph, chart, diagram—something to display statistics. You also need to state what is displayed on the graphic. In this case, you would want to mention what was measured for each game, such as amount and type of physiological response (as noted in question 8). That will earn you 1 of 2 points on this 2-point question. Now you are asked to give two specific examples <u>from the passage</u> that support your choice. You should quote the passage. It would be helpful to mention that since the article discusses measuring heart rate after a 10-minute video, a chart that shows the different rates after various parts of the video are shown would help a reader see what specifically causes the change. Also, you could show which of the video games causes the most response, because readers will likely recognize the names and may be very interested in knowing.

    This sounds like a lot for your 2 points, but it's worth the time to spend to follow the directions exactly and get your 2/2.

11. **(D)** They have discovered, through a study of both men and women, that those who had played violent video games became more numb to the violence they witnessed on television.

    This question sounds tough, but the answer is right in the text. Choice A is incorrect because this wasn't about *reading* research. B discusses acting violent instead of becoming numb to it. C is incorrect because there were no monkeys mentioned in the piece.

12. **(A)** The reader does not expect the author to say, "But the study wasn't over yet," as there were already findings mentioned.

    These questions are rather odd. Choices B and C are incorrect, because those two ideas are exactly what the reader *should* expect to read. D is not logical, considering what's mentioned in paragraph 1 about who is reporting this story. A is best because once findings were mentioned, it appeared that the study had already been concluded.

13. **(B)** Students who had played violent video games showed less physiological response to the real-life videos.

    This question seems to direct you to a specific place in the text, which means you should take the time to go find it and reread the section. Choices A, C, and D are all true statements of fact, so they will look good to you, but choice B describes the findings of the study about "desensitization," so it is the best answer to be used as "evidence."

14. **(C)** "Which medium is most desensitizing: TV, movies, or video games? And are some people more affected than others?"

This one is easy if you take your time and read carefully. They are all mentioned in the passage, so that is no help. Only C is a question that goes unanswered in the passage, making it the best choice with regard to something that's "unclear" to the researchers.

15. **(D)** to become accustomed to a particular situation

Here's another vocabulary question, and it's not too bad if you look carefully at the question and its context. Options B and C don't make sense, so you can exclude those. A is in the ballpark, but the sentence has 'get used to' as a clarifier to the word, so that leaves D as the better of the two.

16. **(A)** A treadmill is a conveyor belt that continues until shut off.

The choices for this one are a bit trickier. Option C uses the word "easy," so it seems not to match the tone of the article. B uses the word "control," and that seems also not to match. Between A and D, A is better because it gives the feeling of endless motion, which is what the author is trying to convey.

17. **(D)** outrageous

This vocabulary question is simple if you plug it into the sentence. The word "impossibility" is used in the previous paragraph in regard to finding a good job and a good place to live after college. So we are looking for high interest rates that make that impossible. With that in mind, D is clearly the best choice. Careful reading and patience would have guaranteed you the right answer here.

18. **(B)** to introduce the essay and set the tone

Typically a note after a title will be used to introduce the piece and show off a little of what the writer is trying to say. Choices C and D are not accurate. A does describe the writer's attitude somewhat, but the word "convince" does not match something like a comment after a title. That's not the place to try to convince a reader.

19. Remember for a summary, you must include all the most important parts in the entire paragraph; don't worry about every single detail. Here are the relevant points in paragraph 4:

-Kids today are very involved.
-Kids today do many things that are designed to make them look better.
-Kids' parents encourage this.
-Previous generations had different views of success.
-Money plays a large role in causing this change.

20. **(B)** the young generation is more interested in their own personal success.

This one is easy if you look back at the passage. The author says that "activist days are gone forever," and then describes today's generation as focusing on their careers.

21. **(C)** the members of the graduating class stop moving.

    Choices A and B are incorrect and somewhat silly. Between C and D, considering the references to a treadmill (see question 16), choice C is the better answer. In the eyes of the author, it seems the constant motion is what causes the problems.

22. **(D)** teens want to be the stars they admire.

    Choice A is simply incorrect. B is too extreme. C is true, but not strong enough given the text. D is accurate and matches the tone of the article. There is much evidence in the text to support that teens actually want to be the stars, not simply admire them.

23. This question has two separate parts, as we discussed in the practice section. Make sure you do both, even using numbers to show that you have addressed each part. A sample answer could be:

    1. In the passage, the word "currency" means general use or accepted use.
    2. A context clue is that the writer follows that sentence with a colon and then goes on to list different tabloids and how they usually have those types of celebrity issues going on, making it typical or "accepted."

    There may be different examples, but remember the word "plausible" or "reasonable" from the scoring rubric. The scorers will be looking to give you credit for offering a response that makes sense and for supporting your example with evidence that matches.

24. **(C)** "In 2006, we found teens who volunteered in locales like Sri Lanka, Guinea and Peru."

    Choices A and B are unrelated to the question. D does not have any connection to giving, as mentioned in the question. This makes C the most obvious answer.

25. **(B)** idea

    This vocabulary question is perfect for the "plug-in" technique. If you substitute the choices into the phrase "further this notion," the clear and obvious correct answer is B. Remember that sometimes you will be required to look back at the passage in addition to examining something provided in the question.

26. **(A)** the teens of the future have a good chance of impacting Hollywood for the better.

    Choices B and C in this one are both poor choices. B is too extreme, and C is perhaps more like an opposite. D has possibilities, but if you think about how the second half of the article changes in tone, A seems a better choice between the two.

27. **(C)** the possibility that some teenagers are looking for instant popularity while others have a clear sense that volunteering is more rewarding.

    This is an interesting set of choices. Option A is out because it is too extreme and specific—the article was not all about eating disorders. B seems the opposite of what the article discusses (see question 26). D may well be inferred from reading the article, but that does not mean the article was all about Angelina Jolie. C is the only choice the matches in topic and in that it covers the entire article.

28. **(C)** Celebrity opinions do not rank as highly as parents, friends, teachers, and the media when it comes to topics such as war and politics.

Keeping in mind that to paraphrase is to restate in different words, you simply need to carefully read each statement and find the one that matches what you were given. Choice A states "dead last," which is too extreme. B changes the question, as does D.

29. Here is another question where you are given a task that is worth four points. You must offer an explanation (1 pt.) and give three examples that support it (3 pts.). Here is a sample response:

Answer: The author does not believe that celebrities are good role models for teens.

1. Teens are willing to make a spectacle of themselves on TV just for attention.
2. Teens pierce their bodies and get tattoos because of celebrities.
3. Teens try to lose weight simply because a celebrity does.

There are other ways to answer this, but note that all four pieces of the required response are present, and the response presents a reasonable answer and evidence to support it.

30. **(B)** that a majority of teenagers model their images after celebrities.

A quick but important look back at paragraph 4 will make it clear that the survey results here show what teens do because of the influence of celebrities. You can exclude C because it's an opposite. D is possible but not mentioned in this article. A is also partially true, but not specific enough to paragraph 4. If you were not careful or if you chose not to look back at paragraph 4, you might have chosen A. Don't make that careless mistake.

31. **(A)** "To avoid arousing unnecessary talk, he took from the table the writing in which the millions were renounced, and when he got home locked it up in the fireproof safe."

This one has a lot of reading, but if you take your time, you'll get the correct answer. Choices B, C, and D all might have come mention or reference to "contempt," but the only one that refers to the banker is A.

32. **(D)** The books he read showed him how money caused the banker to be greedy.

Choice A is incorrect, because there is no support that the lawyer feels he wasted his life. B is likely the opposite of the correct answer. C might be true, but it is not better than D, which is supported by the contents of the lawyer's letter to the banker.

33. **(B)** guilt

    Options C and D are poor choices. The banker does not fail, nor does he not believe what he has seen. While he might feel some relief (A) that the prisoner is gone, the fact that he hides his letter in the safe suggests that he did not want to be caught and face guilt.

34. **(A)** Wealth can be measured in more than monetary value.

    Choice D is rather silly. C might be true, but that was not what the story focused on. B is simply untrue, so it's a poor choice. Considering the lawyer's letter and how he criticizes the banker, A is the best choice.

35. This question asks for four items: an explanation of how the concept of irony is developed and three pieces of evidence from the story to support it. Here is a sample response:

    Answer: In the story, irony is used to show how the lawyer learns more from his bet than he bargained for.

    1. He volunteers to stay in solitary for fifteen years rather than five.
    2. He reads many books but the learning tortures him.
    3. After fifteen years, he leaves hours before he would have won the money.

36. **(D)** It shows the reader that not much has changed despite the experiment.

    Choice A is a true statement, but a bit too simplistic to be the answer. B is untrue, given all that the letter says. C is untrue and rather far-fetched. D is close to something that involves the theme, so it's the best answer.

37. **(C)** lacking in care, judgment, selectivity.

    These choices look similar, so you had to look at the context. The paragraph goes on to describe all of the books he read of different types. No real reason is given for why he chooses them. A is a possibility. B and D are opposites. D is better than A, though, when you consider the context of the paragraph as a whole. But C is the best answer here.

38. **(B)** His thin figure helps to show that he does not feel he needs much of what the outside world has to offer. He is able to live on the bare minimum.

    Choice A is not correct, because there is not a clear connection between sanity and being hunched over. He may be hungry, but there is no evidence he plans to spend his money on food, so C is not the correct answer. D is not logical and does not support the text. B matches the tone of the prisoner's letter.

39. Sample answer:

    The narrator emphasizes the banker's lack of understanding with regard to wealth using the banker's actions during and after the bet.

    1. The banker wastes his money during the bet.
    2. The banker considers killing the prisoner so he does not have to pay.
    3. The banker does not react to the prisoner's letter; he simply hides it.

40. **(A)** Those who have never experienced a struggle cannot understand success.

Consider that *ne'er* means "never," and notice that's next to "succeed." All of this is said by the author to be "sweetest." A is the best choice because it captures that idea exactly. B uses "never," which is too extreme. C uses "ease," which is the opposite idea. D uses a metaphor of battle, which is not indicated in lines 1–4.

41. **(B)** Success often comes after the person has sacrificed for it.

Choice A mentions money, which is not mentioned in the poem. C mentions that one must "feel" successful, which is closer to the opposite idea. D is about battle, but that's too specific for the theme. Battle is used as a metaphor in stanzas 2 and 3.

42. **(C)** Triumph is clear to those who have nearly died for their success.

Choice C is the only answer that includes the idea of sacrifice. D is still referencing the metaphor of battle. A shows a misreading of the poem. B mentions "want," which is not mentioned as an element in the poem.

43. **(A)** He who gains the flag is victorious.

Choice A is the best answer because it matches the metaphor of battling for possession of the flag. Options B, C, and D do not connect well at all.

44. **(C)** show that victory does not come without cost.

Choice A is too specific. B is still stuck in the metaphor of battle. D is too extreme, although it's not beyond a possibility. C is much closer to the theme, and presenting a theme is clearly purposeful.

Reading Practice
ANSWER SHEET—TEST 2

1 Ⓐ Ⓑ Ⓒ Ⓓ

2 Ⓐ Ⓑ Ⓒ Ⓓ

3 Ⓐ Ⓑ Ⓒ Ⓓ

4 Ⓐ Ⓑ Ⓒ Ⓓ

5 Write your response to question 5 in the space below.

_____

_____

_____

_____

_____

_____

_____

_____

_____

_____

_____

_____

_____

6 Ⓐ Ⓑ Ⓒ Ⓓ

7 Ⓐ Ⓑ Ⓒ Ⓓ

8 Ⓐ Ⓑ Ⓒ Ⓓ

9 Ⓐ Ⓑ Ⓒ Ⓓ

10 Write your response to question 10 in the space below.

11 Ⓐ Ⓑ Ⓒ Ⓓ

12 Ⓐ Ⓑ Ⓒ Ⓓ

13 Ⓐ Ⓑ Ⓒ Ⓓ

14 Ⓐ Ⓑ Ⓒ Ⓓ

Reading Practice
ANSWER SHEET—TEST 2

15 (A) (B) (C) (D)

16 (A) (B) (C) (D)

17 (A) (B) (C) (D)

18 (A) (B) (C) (D)

19 Write your response to question 19 in the space below.

20 (A) (B) (C) (D)

21 (A) (B) (C) (D)

22 Ⓐ Ⓑ Ⓒ Ⓓ

23 Write your response to question 23 in the space below.

24 Ⓐ Ⓑ Ⓒ Ⓓ

25 Ⓐ Ⓑ Ⓒ Ⓓ

26 Ⓐ Ⓑ Ⓒ Ⓓ

27 Ⓐ Ⓑ Ⓒ Ⓓ

Reading Practice
ANSWER SHEET—TEST 2

28 Ⓐ Ⓑ Ⓒ Ⓓ

29 Write your response to question 29 in the space below.

30 Ⓐ Ⓑ Ⓒ Ⓓ

31 Ⓐ Ⓑ Ⓒ Ⓓ

32 Ⓐ Ⓑ Ⓒ Ⓓ

33 Ⓐ Ⓑ Ⓒ Ⓓ

34 Ⓐ Ⓑ Ⓒ Ⓓ

35 Write your response to question 35 in the space below.

36 Ⓐ Ⓑ Ⓒ Ⓓ

37 Ⓐ Ⓑ Ⓒ Ⓓ

38 Ⓐ Ⓑ Ⓒ Ⓓ

Reading Practice
ANSWER SHEET–TEST 2

39 Write your response to question 39 in the space below.

_____

_____

_____

_____

_____

_____

_____

_____

_____

_____

_____

_____

_____

_____

40 Ⓐ Ⓑ Ⓒ Ⓓ

41 Ⓐ Ⓑ Ⓒ Ⓓ

42 Ⓐ Ⓑ Ⓒ Ⓓ

43 Ⓐ Ⓑ Ⓒ Ⓓ

44 Ⓐ Ⓑ Ⓒ Ⓓ

Reading Practice

Reading Practice Test 2

Directions: Each passage in this test is followed by several questions. After reading the passage, choose the correct answer for each multiple-choice question, and then mark the corresponding circle in the Answer Document. If you change an answer, be sure to erase the first mark completely.

For the written-response questions, answer completely in the Answer Document in the space provided. You may not need to use the entire space provided.

You may refer to the passages as often as necessary. Make sure the number of the question in this test booklet corresponds to the number on the Answer Document. Be sure all your answers are complete and appear in the Answer Document.

Clayton Holbert

Ottawa, Kansas

Interviewed by Leta Gray

1 "My name is Clayton Holbert, and I am an ex-slave. I am eighty-six years old. I was born and raised in Linn County, Tennessee. My master's name was Pleasant "Ples" Holbert. My master had a fairly large plantation; he had, I imagine, around one hundred slaves."

2 "I was working the fields during the wind-up of the Civil War. They always had a man in the field to teach the small boys to work, and I was one of the boys. I was learning to plant corn, etc. My father, brother and uncle went to war on the Union side."

3 "We raised corn, barley, and cotton, and produced all of our living on the plantation. There was no such thing as going to town to buy things. All of our clothing was homespun, our socks were knitted, and everything. We had our looms, and made our own suits, we also had reels, and we carved, spun, and knitted. We always wore yarn socks for winter, which we made.

It didn't get cold, in the winter in Tennessee, just a little frost was all. We fixed all of our cotton and wool ourselves."

4 "For our meat we used to kill fifteen, twenty, or fifty, and sometimes a hundred hogs. We usually had hickory. It was considered the best for smoking meat, when we butchered. Our meat we had then was the finest possible. It had a lot more flavor than that which you get now. If a person ran out of meat, he would go over to his neighbor's house, and borrow or buy meat, we didn't think about going to town. When we wanted fresh meat we or some of the neighbors would kill a hog or sheep, and would divide this, and then when we butchered we would give them part of ours. People were more friendly than they are now. They have almost lost respect for each other. Now if you would give your neighbor something they would never think of paying it back. You could also borrow wheat or whatever you wanted, and you could pay it back whenever you thrashed."

5 "We also made our own sorghum, dried our own fruits. We usually dried all of our things as we never heard of such a thing as canning."

6 "We always had brandy, wine, and cider on hand, and nothing was thought of it. We used to give it to the children even. When we had corn husks; log rolling, etc., we would invite all of the neighbors over, and then we would serve refreshments of wine, brandy or cider."

7 "We made our own maple syrup from the maple sugar trees. This is a lot better than the refined sugar people have nowdays, and is good for you too. You can't get this now though, except sometimes and it is awfully high priced. On the plantations the slaves usually had a house of their own for their families. They usually built their houses in a circle, so you didn't have to go out doors hardly to go to the house next to you. If you wanted your house away from the rest of the houses, they could build you a house away from the others and separate. I was never sold, I always had just my one master. When slave owners died, if they had no near relatives to inherit their property, they would 'Will' the slaves their freedom, instead of giving them to someone else. My grandmother, and my mother were both freed like this, but what they called 'traders' captured them and two or three others, and they took them just like they would animals, and sold them, that was how 'Ples' Holbert got my mother. My grandmother was sent to Texas. My mother said she wrote and had one letter from my grandmother after that, but she never saw her again."

8 "My mother used to be a cook, and when she was busy cooking, my mistress would nurse both me and her baby, who was four weeks older than me. If it happened the other way around, my mother would nurse both of us. They didn't think anything about it. When the old people died, and they left small orphan children, the slaves would raise the children. My young master was raised like this, he has written to me several times, since I have been out here in Kansas, but the last time I wrote, I have had no reply, so I suppose he was dead."

9 "When anyone died, they used to bury the body at least six feet under the ground. There wasn't such a thing as a cemetery then, they were just buried right on the plantation, usually close to the house. They would put the body

in a wagon, and walk to where to bury the person, and they would sing all of the way."

10 "The slaves used to dance or go to the prayer meeting to pass their time. There were also festivals we went to, during the Christmas vacation. There was always a big celebration on Christmas. We worked until Christmas Eve and from that time until New Year's we had a vacation. We had no such thing as Thanksgiving, we had never heard of such a thing."

11 "In August when it was the hottest we always had a vacation after our crops were all laid by. That was the time when we usually had several picnics, barbecues or anything we wanted to do to pass our time away."

12 "After the war was over, and my father, brother and uncle had gone to war, it left my mother alone practically. My mother had always been a cook, and that was all she knew, and after the war she got her freedom, she and me, I was seven or eight years old, and my brother was fourteen, and my sister was about sixteen. My mother didn't know what to do, and I guess we looked kind of pitiful, finally my master said that we could stay and work for him a year, and then we also stayed there the following year, and he paid us the second year. After that we went to another place, Roof Macaroy, and then my sister got married while we were there, and then she moved on her husband's master's place, and then we went too. After that I moved on another part and farmed for two or three years, and then we moved to another part of the plantation and lived there three or four years. That was almost the center of things, and we held church there. All of the colored people would gather there. The colored people who had been in the North were better educated than the people in the South. They would come down to the South and help the rest of us. The white people would also try to promote religion among the colored people. Our church was a big log cabin. We lived in it, but we moved from one of the large rooms into a small one, so we could have church. I remember one time after we had been down on the creek bank fishing, that was what we always did on Sunday, because we didn't know any better; my master called us boys and told us we should go to Sunday school instead of going fishing. I remember that to this day, and I have only been fishing one or two times since. Then I didn't know what he was talking about, but two or three years later I learned what Sunday school was, and I started to go."

13 "I went to a subscription school. We would all pay a man to come to teach us. I used to work for my room and board on Saturday's, and go to school five days a week. That would have been all right, if I had kept it up, but I didn't for very long, I learned to read and write pretty good though. There were no Government schools then that were free."

14 "We didn't have a name. The slaves were always known by the master's last name, and after we were freed we just took the last name of our masters and used it. After we had got our freedom papers, they had our ages and all on them, they were lost so we guess at our ages."

15 "Most of the slave owners were good to their slaves although some of them were brutish of course."

16 "In 1877 a lot of people began coming out here to Kansas and in 1878 there were several, but in 1879 there were an awful lot of colored people immigrating. We came in 1877 to Kansas City, October 1. We landed about midnight. We came by train. Then there was nothing but little huts in the bottoms. The Santa Fe depot didn't amount to anything. The Armours' Packing house was ever smaller than that. There was a swinging bridge over the river. The Raw Valley was considered good-for-nothing, but to raise hemp. There was an awful lot of it grown there though, and there were also beavers in the Kaw River, and they used to cut down trees to build their dams. I worked several years and in 1890 I came to Franklin County."

17 "We raised a lot of corn, and castor beans. That was the money crop. Corn at that time wasn't hard to raise. People never plowed their corn more than three times, and they got from forty to fifty bushels per acre. There were no weeds and it was virgin soil. One year I got seventy-two bushel of corn per acre, and I just plowed it once. That may sound 'fishy' but it is true."

18 "There used to be a castor bean mill here, and I have seen the wagons of castor beans lined from Logan Street to First Street, waiting to unload. They had to number the wagons to avoid trouble and they made them keep their places. There also used to be a water mill here, but it burned."

19 "There were lots of Indians here in the Chippewas. They were harmless though. They were great to come in town, and shoot for pennies. They were good shots, and it kept you going to keep them supplied with pennies for them to shoot with their bows and arrows, as they almost always hit them. They were always dressed in their red blankets."

20 "I have never used ones for work. They were used quite a bit, although I have never used them. They were considered to be good after they were broken."

21 "I was about twenty-two years old when I married, and I have raised six children. They live over by Appanoose. I ruined my health hauling wood. I was always a big fellow, I used to weigh over two hundred eighty-five pounds, but I worked too hard, working both summer and winter."

22 "My father's mother lived 'till she was around ninety or a hundred years old. She got so bent at the last she was practically bent double. She lived about two years after she was set free."

23 "I used to live up around Appanoose, but I came to Franklin County and I have stayed here ever since."

Leta Gray (Interviewer) May 17, 1937 for *The American Guide*, Topeka, Kansas. Person interviewed in Ottawa, Kansas. Source: *The American Slave*, Supp. Series 2, Vol. 1: 285–291. (http://xroads.virginia.edu/~hyper/wpa/holbert1.html)

1. This account of a man's life growing up as a slave is an example of

    A. a compare and contrast essay
    B. a narrative essay
    C. a persuasive essay
    D. a descriptive essay

2. To find out when the term "subscription school" first entered the English language, where would you look for this type of information?

   A. dictionary
   B. thesaurus
   C. almanac
   D. atlas

3. The author suggests that his feelings of the current relationships between neighbors is:

   A. one that has stayed the same, people trade with each other and return favors.
   B. one that has changed, people trade with each other and return favors.
   C. one that has changed, people no longer trade or return favors.
   D. one that has stayed the same, people never traded or returned favors.

4. The author includes the scenario of his father's mother to show

   A. that despite any hardships he or his family had had, his family members lived a long time.
   B. that his father's mother had a hard life and his life was just as hard.
   C. that there are very few similarities between he and his family members because he was never around them.
   D. that he was not as healthy as his father's mother.

5. Explain what the author means when he says, "People were more friendly than they are now. They have almost lost respect for each other. Now if you would give your neighbor something they would never think of paying it back. You could also borrow wheat or whatever you wanted, and you could pay it back whenever you thrashed," and give a detail or example from the passage to support your idea. Write your answer in the space provided on the Answer Sheet. (2 points)

6. Which most closely describes the author's reasons for writing this piece?

   A. To compare what it was like to be raised as a slave and contrast it with how people are raised today.
   B. To describe what it felt like to grow up a slave.
   C. To narrate his own personal account as a slave.
   D. To help people understand American History.

Soccer: History and Development

1 Games revolving around the kicking of a ball have been played in many countries throughout history. According to FIFA, the "very earliest form of the game for which there is scientific evidence was an exercise of precisely this skilful technique dating back to the 2nd and 3rd centuries B.C. in China."[3] In addition, the Roman games *Harpastum* may be a distant ancestor of football [soccer]. Various forms of football were played in medieval Europe, though rules varied greatly by both period and location.

2 Whilst football has continued to be played in various forms throughout Britain, the English public schools (fee-paying schools) are widely credited with certain key achievements in the creation of modern football (association football and the rugby football games - rugby league and rugby union football). The evidence suggests that during the sixteenth century English public schools generally, and headmaster Richard Mulcaster in particular, were instrumental in taking football away from its violent "mob" form and turning it into an organised team sport that was beneficial to schoolboys. Therefore, the game became institutionalised, regulated, and part of a larger, more central tradition. Many early descriptions of football and references to it (e.g., poetry) were recorded by people who had studied at these schools, showing they were familiar with the game. Finally, in the 19th century, teachers and former students were the first to write down formal rules of early modern football to enable matches to be played between schools.

3 The rules of football as they are <u>codified</u> today are effectively based on the mid-19th-century efforts to standardise the widely varying forms of football played at the public schools of England. The first ever set of football rules were written at Eton College in 1815. The Cambridge Rules were a code of football rules, first drawn up at Cambridge University in 1848, which have influenced the development of Association football (also known simply as "football", or soccer) and subsequent codes.

4 The Cambridge Rules were written at Trinity College, Cambridge in 1848, at a meeting attended by representatives from Eton, Harrow, Rugby, Winchester and Shrewsbury schools, but they were not universally <u>adopted</u>. During the 1850s, many clubs unconnected to schools or universities were formed throughout the English-speaking world to play various forms of football. Some came up with their own distinct codes of rules, most notably the Sheffield Football Club (formed by former pupils from Harrow) in 1857, which led to formation of a Sheffield FA in 1867. In 1862, John Charles Thring of Uppingham School also devised an influential set of rules.[4]

5 These ongoing efforts contributed to the formation of The Football Association (The FA) in 1863 which first met on the morning of 26 October 1863 at the Freemason's Tavern in Great Queen Street, London.[5] The only school to be represented on this occasion was Charterhouse. The Freemason's Tavern was the setting for five more meetings between October and December, which eventually produced the first comprehensive set of rules. At the final meeting, the first FA treasurer, the representative from Blackheath, withdrew his club from the FA over the removal of two draft rules at the previous meeting, the first which allowed for the running with the ball in hand and the second, obstructing such a run by hacking (kicking an opponent in the shins), tripping and holding. Other English rugby clubs followed this lead and did not join the FA but instead in 1871 formed the Rugby Football Union. The eleven remaining clubs, under the charge of Ebenezer Cobb Morley, went on to ratify the original thirteen laws of the game. The Sheffield FA played by its own rules until the 1870s.

6 The laws of the game are currently determined by the International Football Association Board (IFAB). The Board was formed in 1886[6] after a meeting in Manchester of The Football Association, the Scottish Football Association, the Football Association of Wales, and the Irish Football Association. The world's oldest football competition is the FA Cup, which was founded by C. W. Alcock and has been contested by English teams since 1872. The first official international football match took place in 1872 between Scotland and England in Glasgow, again at the instigation of C. W. Alcock. England is home to the world's first football league, which was founded in 1888 by Aston Villa director William McGregor.[7] The original format contained 12 clubs from the Midlands and the North of England. The Fédération Internationale de Football Association (FIFA), the international football body, was formed in Paris in 1904 and declared that they would adhere to Laws of the Game of the Football Association.[8] The growing popularity of the international game led to the admittance of FIFA representatives to the International Football Association Board in 1913. The board currently consists of four representatives from FIFA and one representative from each of the four British associations.

7 Today, football is played at a professional level all over the world, and millions of people regularly go to football stadia to follow their favourite team,[9] whilst billions more watch the game on television.[10] A very large number of people also play football at an amateur level. According to a survey conducted by FIFA and published in the spring of 2001, over 240 million people regularly play football in more than 200 countries in every part of the world.[11] Its simple rules and minimal equipment requirements have no doubt aided its spread and growth in popularity.

8 In many parts of the world football evokes great passions and plays an important role in the life of individual fans, local communities, and even nations; it is therefore often claimed to be the most popular sport in the world. ESPN has spread the claim that the Côte d'Ivoire national football team helped secure a truce to the nation's civil war in 2005. By contrast, however, football is widely considered to be the final proximate cause in the Football War in June 1969 between El Salvador and Honduras. The sport also exacerbated tensions at the beginning of the Yugoslav wars of the 1990s, when a Red Star Belgrade-at-Dinamo Zagreb match devolved into rioting in March 1990.[12]

References

1. 2002 FIFA World Cup TV Coverage, FIFA official website. Retrieved on May 13, 2006.
2. The World's Most Beloved Sport - The History of Soccer. *fussballportal.de*. Retrieved on June 3, 2006.
3. England Premiership (2005/2006). *Sportpress*. Retrieved on June 5, 2006.
4. History of Football. *FIFA*. Retrieved on 20 November 2006.
5. The hands-off approach to a man's game. *The Times*. Retrieved on June 3, 2006.

6. History of the FA. Football Association website. Retrieved on February 19, 2006.

7. The International FA Board. FIFA website. Retrieved on February 19, 2006.

8. The History Of The Football League. Football League website. Retrieved on April 19, 2006.

9. History of FIFA. FIFA website. Retrieved on June 3, 2006.

10. Baseball or Football: which sport gets the higher attendance?, *Guardian Unlimited*. Retrieved on June 5, 2006.

11. 2002 FIFA World Cup TV Coverage. FIFA official website. Retrieved on May 13, 2006.

12. FIFA Survey: approximately 250 million footballers worldwide. FIFA official website. Retrieved on June 5, 2006.

13. Daniel W. Drezner. "The Soccer Wars." *The Washington Post*, Sunday, June 4, 2006, p. B01.

14. The Official web site of the Fédération Internationale de Football Association. Retrieved on 2006–04-19.

15. The History of Offside. *Julian Carosi*. Retrieved on June 3, 2006.

16. FIFA World Cup 2006. FIFA World Cup 2006 website. Retrieved on February 19, 2006.

17. Where it all began. FIFA official website. Retrieved on April 10, 2006.

18. Football - An Olympic Sport since 1900. IOC website. Retrieved on June 5, 2006.

(http://en.wikipedia)

7. Which technique does the author use to have readers view the information in the article as credible?

A. The author makes clear that he is gathering information from outside sources, further citing information from soccer associations.

B. The author is a member of a soccer association.

C. The author expresses surprise at how popular soccer has become.

D. The author struggles with summarizing difficult soccer terms and plays.

8. The author incorporates many terms in the passage. Which definition means the same as <u>codified</u>?

A. to make more exciting

B. to shorten

C. to reduce laws, rules, etc. to a code

D. to create a code only those who play understand

9. Which statement represents the main idea of the article?

   A. Football (soccer) is only popular in Europe.
   B. The rules of football (soccer) are different in every country since the beginning of time.
   C. Not only is football (soccer) a popular sport unifying its fans, but it has been around for a number of years, undergoing an evolution into what it is today.
   D. American football and international football are not the same.

10. Describe a picture or other graphic that would help a reader more clearly understand or be more interested in the ideas given in the passage. Give two specific examples from the passage that support your choice of a picture or other graphic. Write your answer in the space provided on the Answer Sheet. (2 points)

11. How does the researcher know that soccer dates back to the 2nd and 3rd centuries B.C.?

    A. The researcher has observed the practices of soccer and noticed similarities in the wall pictures left behind in caves.
    B. The researcher has interviewed people from FIFA.
    C. The researcher has done research using a variety of sources.
    D. The researcher plays soccer and has heard the stories passed on from generations prior.

12. How does the author surprise the reader?

    A. The author mentions that soccer's simple rules and minimal equipment requirements have no doubt aided its spread and growth in popularity.
    B. The reader does not expect to see that football has grown in its popularity because it has colorful uniforms that people find attractive.
    C. The reader does not expect to see that football is widely considered to be the final proximate cause in the Football War in June 1969 between El Salvador and Honduras.
    D. The reader does not expect to see many people have a favorite team in football.

13. What was the evidence presented in the passage of soccer having evolved over time?

    A. The game began in the 2nd and 3rd centuries. However, the rules have changed because no one could agree on one set of rules.
    B. The game began in the 2nd and 3rd centuries. However, the rules have changed to make it easier to play.
    C. The game began in the 2nd and 3rd centuries. However, the rules changed because girls wanted to play, too.
    D. The game began in the 2nd and 3rd centuries. However, the rules have changed from a disorderly sport, to a more regulated sport.

14. What evidence does the author present for the notion that soccer has affected many people today?

    A. According to a survey conducted by FIFA and published in the spring of 2001, over 240 million people regularly play football in more than 200 countries in every part of the world.

    B. The growing popularity of the international game led to the admittance of FIFA representatives to the International Football Association Board in 1913.

    C. Soccer is a sport anyone can play due to the simplicity of its rules.

    D. Soccer has begun wars, and soccer has ended wars.

15. Which definition means the same as <u>adopted</u> does in this sentence "The Cambridge Rules were written at Trinity College, Cambridge in 1848, at a meeting attended by representatives from Eton, Harrow, Rugby, Winchester and Shrewsbury schools, but they were not universally adopted" from paragraph 4?

    A. to take into one's family by legal means and raise as one's own child

    B. to correct

    C. to change because of disagreement

    D. to choose as a standard or required in a course

PUPPIES FOR SALE

1 A farmer had some puppies he needed to sell. He painted a sign advertising the pups and set about nailing it to a post on the edge of his yard. As he was driving the last nail into the post, he felt a tug on his overalls. He looked down into the eyes of a little boy.

2 "Mister," he said, "I want to buy one of your puppies."

3 "Well," said the farmer, as he rubbed the sweat off the back of his neck, "these puppies come from fine parents and cost a good deal of money."

4 The boy dropped his head for a moment. Then reaching deep into his pocket, he pulled out a handful of change and held it up to the farmer. "I've got thirty-nine cents. Is that enough to take a look?"

5 "Sure," said the farmer. And with that he let out a whistle. "Here, Dolly!" he called.

6 Out from the doghouse and down the ramp ran Dolly followed by four little balls of fur. The little boy pressed his face against the chain link fence. His eyes danced with delight.

7 As the dogs made their way to the fence, the little boy noticed something else stirring inside the doghouse. Slowly another little ball appeared; this one noticeably smaller. Down the ramp it slid. Then in a somewhat <u>awkward</u> manner the little pup began hobbling toward the others, doing its best to catch up . . . .

8 "I want that one," the little boy said, pointing to the runt.

9 The farmer knelt down at the boy's side and said, "Son, you don't want that puppy. He will never be able to run and play with you like these other dogs would."

10 With that the little boy stepped back from the fence, reached down, and began rolling up one leg of his trousers. In doing so he revealed a steel brace running down both sides of his leg attaching itself to a specially made shoe. Looking back up at the farmer, he said, "You see sir, I don't run too well myself, and he will need someone who understands."

11 The world is full of people who need someone who understands.

(http://www.indianchild.com/puppies_for_sale.htm)

16. The author compares the puppy and the boy. Why is that?

    A. The puppy and the boy are both cute, and they will be perfect for each other.

    B. The puppy and the boy are not wanted, and that is why they will want each other.

    C. The puppy hobbles, and the boy has a leg brace. They will understand each other.

    D. The puppy is awkward, and the boy is mature; the boy will be able to understand the puppy's disability because of his maturity.

17. Which word represents the meaning of <u>awkward</u> as used in paragraph 7?

    A. happy

    B. young

    C. rough

    D. ungraceful

18. What is the purpose of the sentence "With that the little boy stepped back from the fence, reached down, and began rolling up one leg of his trousers"?

    A. to provide irony to the story

    B. to provide background information to the story

    C. to provide a climax to the story

    D. to provide the resolution to the story

19. Summarize paragraph 10. Write the answer in the space provided on the Answer Sheet. (2 points)

20. The farmer says, "Son, you don't want that puppy." He says this because

    A. the puppy will not be able to "run and play like the other dogs would."

    B. the puppy is not well behaved.

    C. the puppy is too expensive because it comes from "fine parents."

    D. the puppy is always last.

21. According to the author, "The world is full of people . . ."

   A. who will give a little boy a puppy because he understands it.
   B. who dislike dogs that cannot run and play.
   C. who need a puppy.
   D. who need someone who understands.

1 Because I could not stop for Death,
    He kindly stopped for me;
    The carriage held but just ourselves
    And Immortality.

2 We slowly drove, he knew no <u>haste</u>,
    And I had put away
    My labor, and my leisure too,
    For his civility.

3 We passed the school, where children strove
    At recess, in the ring;
    We passed the fields of gazing grain,
    We passed the setting sun.

4 Or rather, he passed us;
    The dews grew quivering and chill,
    For only <u>gossamer</u> my gown,
    My tippet only tulle.

5 We paused before house that seemed
    A swelling of the ground;
    The roof was scarcely visible,
    The cornice but a mound.

6 Since then 'tis centuries, and yet each
    Feels shorter than the day
    I first surmised the horses' heads
    Were toward eternity.

Emily Dickinson
(http://academic.brooklyn.cuny.edu/english/melani/cs6/stop.html)

22. The author suggests

   A. there are many things to see when riding with Death.
   B. death is not very friendly to any man or woman.
   C. no man or woman escapes death.
   D. death does not escape any man or woman.

23. Using the poem as a guide, define the word <u>haste</u>. Give a context clue from the passage that helped you come to your definition. Write your answer in the space provided on the Answer Sheet. (2 points)

24. Which quotation supports the author's view that no man or woman escapes death?

    A. "We slowly drove, he knew no haste, / And I had put away / My labor, and my leisure too, / For his civility."
    B. "Since then 'tis centuries, and yet each / Feels shorter than the day."
    C. "The roof was scarcely visible / The cornice but a mound."
    D. "Because I could not stop for Death, / He kindly stopped for me;"

25. Which definition most closely means <u>gossamer</u> as used in the quotation "The dews grew quivering and chill, / For only gossamer my gown"?

    A. any thin, light fabric
    B. a heavy, thick fabric
    C. a black fabric worn in death
    D. a white fabric that brides wear

26. According to the poem, the author feels that

    A. death is not very civil.
    B. death is very scary.
    C. death is eternal.
    D. death is unavoidable.

27. This passage is about

    A. someone who died as a child playing on the playground.
    B. the observations of the poet during a near death experience. Luckily, she escaped death.
    C. the observations of a someone dying. He/She is taken by death; he/she observes life going on without him/her. Then he/she finally rests in the ground in his/her grave.
    D. the observations of Death coming for someone. Death takes him/her. Death observes life going on without him/her. Then finally, Death lays the person to rest in his/her grave.

28. "We paused before house that seemed / A swelling of the ground; / the roof was scarcely visible, / The cornice but a mound."

    This sentence from stanza 5 can be paraphrased as

    A. the narrator's home is a mound of dirt with a broken roof.
    B. the narrator's final "home" is the grave.
    C. the narrator's home has been turned to dust.
    D. the narrator is mistaking the hills of England for his/her home.

29. Explain how the author has shown proof that the speaker feels death is an unavoidable experience. Support your explanation by giving three examples or details from the passage. Write your answer in the space provided on the Answer Sheet. (4 points)

30. The author includes a description of Death by saying he put away his "labor and leisure too, for his civility" in order to show

    A. death is very quick.
    B. death is to be feared.
    C. death is courteous.
    D. death is scary and harsh.

The Mouse
by SAKI (H. H. MUNRO)

1   THEODORIC VOLER HAD been brought up, from infancy to the confines of middle age, by a fond mother whose chief solicitude had been to keep him screened from what she called the coarser realities of life. When she died she left Theodoric alone in a world that was as real as ever, and a good deal coarser than he considered it had any need to be. To a man of his temperament and upbringing even a simple railway journey was crammed with petty annoyances and minor discords, and as he settled himself down in a second-class compartment one September morning he was conscious of ruffled feelings and general mental discomposure. He had been staying at a country vicarage, the inmates of which had been certainly neither brutal nor bacchanalian,* but their supervision of the domestic establishment had been of that lax order which invites disaster. The pony carriage that was to take him to the station had never been properly ordered, and when the moment for his departure drew near, the handyman who should have produced the required article was nowhere to be found. In this emergency Theodoric, to his mute but very intense disgust, found himself obliged to collaborate with the vicar's daughter in the task of harnessing the pony, which necessitated groping about in an ill-lighted outbuilding called a stable, and smelling very like one—except in patches where it smelled of mice. Without being actually afraid of mice, Theodoric classed them among the coarser incidents of life, and considered that Providence, with a little exercise of moral courage, might long ago have recognized that they were not indispensable, and have withdrawn them from circulation. As the train glided out of the station Theodoric's nervous imagination accused himself of exhaling a weak odor of stable yard, and possibly of displaying a moldy straw or two on his unusually well-brushed garments. Fortunately the only other occupation of the compartment, a lady of about the same age as himself, seemed inclined for slumber rather than scrutiny; the train was not due to stop till the terminus was reached, in about an hour's time, and the carriage was of the old-fashioned sort that held no communication with a corridor, therefore no further traveling companions were likely to intrude on Theodoric's semiprivacy. And yet the train had scarcely attained its normal speed before he became reluctantly but vividly aware that he was not alone with the slumbering lady; he was not even alone in his own clothes. A warm, creeping movement over his flesh betrayed the unwelcome and highly resented presence, unseen but poignant, of a strayed mouse, that had evidently dashed into its present retreat during

*bacchanalian: a boisterous festivity

the episode of the pony harnessing. Furtive stamps and shakes and wildly directed pinches failed to dislodge the intruder, whose motto, indeed, seemed to be Excelsior; and the lawful occupant of the clothes lay back against the cushions and endeavored rapidly to evolve some means for putting an end to the dual ownership. It was unthinkable that he should continue for the space of a whole hour in the horrible position of a Rowton House for vagrant mice (already his imagination had at least doubled the numbers of the alien invasion). On the other hand, nothing less drastic than partial disrobing would ease him of his tormentor, and to undress in the presence of a lady, even for so laudable a purpose, was an idea that made his ear tips tingle in a blush of abject shame. He had never been able to bring himself even to the mild exposure of openwork socks in the presence of the fair sex. And yet—the lady in this case was to all appearances soundly and securely asleep; the mouse, on the other hand, seemed to be trying to crowd a wanderjahr into a few strenuous minutes. If there is any truth in the theory of transmigration, this particular mouse must certainly have been in a former state a member of the Alpine Club. Sometimes in its eagerness it lost its footing and slipped for half an inch or so; and then, in fright, or more probably temper, it bit. Theodoric was goaded into the most <u>audacious</u> undertaking of his life. Crimsoning to the hue of a beetroot and keeping an agonized watch on his slumbering fellow traveler, he swiftly and noiselessly secured the ends of his railway rug to the racks on either side of the carriage, so that a substantial curtain hung athwart the compartment. In the narrow dressing room that he had thus improvised he proceeded with violent haste to extricate himself partially and the mouse entirely from the surrounding casings of tweed and half-wool. As the unraveled mouse gave a wild leap to the floor, the rug, slipping its fastening at either end, also came down with a heart-curdling flop, and almost simultaneously the awakened sleeper opened her eyes. With a movement almost quicker than the mouse's, Theodoric pounced on the rug and hauled its ample folds chin-high over his dismantled person as he collapsed into the farther corner of the carriage. The blood raced and beat in the veins of his neck and forehead, while he waited dumbly for the communication cord to be pulled. The lady, however, contented herself with a silent stare at her strangely muffled companion. How much had she seen, Theodoric queried to himself; and in any case what on earth must she think of his present posture?

2 "I think I have caught a chill," he ventured desperately.

3 "Really, I'm sorry," she replied. "I was just going to ask you if you would open this window."

4 "I fancy it's malaria," he added, his teeth chattering slightly, as much from fright as from a desire to support his theory.

5 "I've got some brandy in my holdall, if you'll kindly reach it down for me," said his companion.

6 "Not for worlds—I mean, I never take anything for it," he assured her earnestly.

7 "I suppose you caught it in the tropics?"

8   Theodoric, whose acquaintance with the tropics was limited to an annual present of a chest of tea from an uncle in Ceylon, felt that even the malaria was slipping from him. Would it be possible, he wondered to disclose the real state of affairs to her in small installments?

9   "Are you afraid of mice?" he ventured, growing, if possible, more scarlet in the face.

10   "Not unless they came in quantities. Why do you ask?"

11   "I had one crawling inside my clothes just now," said Theodoric in a voice that hardly seemed his own. "It was a most awkward situation."

12   "It must have been, if you wear your clothes at all tight," she observed. "But mice have strange ideas of comfort."

13   "I had to get rid of it while you were asleep," he continued. Then, with a gulp, he added, "It was getting rid of it that brought me to-to this."

14   "Surely leaving off one small mouse wouldn't bring on a chill," she exclaimed, with a levity that Theodoric accounted abominable.

15   Evidently she had detected something of his predicament, and was enjoying his confusion. All the blood in his body seemed to have mobilized in one concentrated blush, and an agony of abasement, worse than a myriad mice, crept up and down over his soul. And then, as reflection began to assert itself, sheer terror took the place of humiliation. With every minute that passed the train was rushing nearer to the crowded and bustling terminus, where dozens of prying eyes would be exchanged for the one paralyzing pair that watched him from the farther corner of the carriage. There was one slender, despairing chance, which the next few minutes must decide. His fellow traveler might relapse into a blessed slumber. But as the minutes throbbed by that chance ebbed away. The furtive glance which Theodoric stole at her from time to time disclosed only an unwinking wakefulness.

16   "I think we must be getting near now," she presently observed.

17   Theodoric had already noted with growing terror the recurring stacks of small, ugly dwellings that heralded the journey's end. The words acted as a signal. Like a hunted beast breaking cover and dashing madly toward some other haven of momentary safety he threw aside his rug, and struggled frantically into his disheveled garments. He was conscious of dull suburban stations racing past the window, of a choking, hammering sensation in his throat and heart, and of an icy silence in that corner toward which he dared not look. Then as he sank back in his seat, clothed and almost delirious, the train slowed down to a final crawl, and the woman spoke.

18   "Would you be so kind," she asked, "as to get me a porter to put me into a cab? It's a shame to trouble you when you're feeling unwell, but being blind makes one so helpless at a railway station."

(http://www.classicshorts.com/stories/mouse.html)

31. Which of the excerpts illustrates Theodoric's own helplessness?

    A. Theodoric had already noted with growing terror the recurring stacks of small, ugly dwellings that heralded the journey's end. The words acted as a signal. Like a hunted beast breaking cover and dashing madly toward some other haven of momentary safety he threw aside his rug, and struggled frantically into his disheveled garments.

    B. "Are you afraid of mice?" he ventured, growing, if possible, more scarlet in the face.

    C. "Would you be so kind," she asked, "as to get me a porter to put me into a cab? It's a shame to trouble you when you're feeling unwell, but being blind makes one so helpless at a railway station."

    D. "Surely leaving off one small mouse wouldn't bring on a chill," she exclaimed, with a levity that Theodoric accounted abominable.

32. Why did the woman stare at Theodoric with "unwinking wakefulness"?

    A. She is blind.
    B. She is stoic.
    C. She is unkind.
    D. She is flirting.

33. Which word best describes the tone of paragraph 17?

    A. indifferent
    B. angry
    C. happy
    D. fearful

34. Which of the statements below describes a theme from the story?

    A. Jumping to conclusions can create the wrong conclusions.
    B. Being afraid is nothing to fear.
    C. Everyone has a disability.
    D. Everyone must overcome a fear.

35. Explain how the concept of suspense is developed throughout the story. Use three examples from the story to support your answer. Write your answer in the space provided on the Answer Sheet. (4 points)

36. What was the author's purpose in telling the reader about Theodoric's experience in the stable?

    A. to explain why mice try to hide in a person's clothing
    B. to explain why the woman was not afraid of the mouse
    C. to explain how the mouse arrived onto the train
    D. to explain how unhappy Theodoric was at the inconvenience of having to go into the stable

37. Based on the information provided in paragraph 1, <u>audacious</u> means

    A. extremely persuasive; recklessly deceitful.
    B. extremely happy; recklessly jovial.
    C. extremely disrespectful; bordering rudeness.
    D. extremely bold or daring; recklessly brave.

38. In paragraph 1, how does the image of Theodoric hauling the rug's "ample folds chin-high over his dismantled person as he collapsed into the farther corner of the carriage" contribute to the reader's perception of Theodoric's character?

    A. It shows that he is brave for getting rid of the mouse.
    B. It shows he is afraid of the smallest problems in life.
    C. It shows he has been so sheltered from "the real world" that he doesn't know how to kill a mouse.
    D. It shows he has no understanding of how to behave around people with disabilities.

39. Explain how Theodoric's behavior emphasizes his misunderstanding of the "realities of life." Use information from the story to support your answer. Write your response in the space provided on the Answer Sheet. (4 points)

OZYMANDIAS
By Percy Bysshe Shelley

1   I met a traveller from an antique land
    Who said: `Two vast and trunkless legs of stone
    Stand in the desert. Near them, on the sand,
    Half sunk, a shattered visage lies, whose frown,

5   And wrinkled lip, and sneer of cold command,
    Tell that its sculptor well those passions read
    Which yet survive, stamped on these lifeless things,
    The hand that mocked them and the heart that fed.
    And on the pedestal these words appear—

10   "My name is Ozymandias, king of kings:
    Look on my works, ye Mighty, and despair!"
    Nothing beside remains. Round the decay
    Of that colossal wreck, boundless and bare

14   The lone and level sands stretch far away.

(http://poetry.eserver.org/ozymandias.txt)

40. Based on the information in lines 3–7, which sentence gives the best interpretation of that passage?

   A. The sculptor met a similar fate as that of the sculpture he created.
   B. The sneer and wrinkled lip will be remembered more than the great deeds Ozymandias feels he accomplished.
   C. Part of the sculpture is buried in the sand, as is the sculptor.
   D. The sculptor couldn't create something that outlasted time.

41. Which best represents the theme of the poem?

   A. Everything becomes dust in the end.
   B. Regardless of the empire created, it will eventually crack.
   C. Nothing lasts forever in the desert.
   D. Ozymandias was an arrogant and mean ruler.

42. In the last lines of the poem the author says "Round the decay / Of that colossal wreck, boundless and bare / The lone and level sands stretch far away."

   Which sentence represents his intended meaning?

   A. The broken sculpture is living in despair in the desert.
   B. The desert is bigger than the fallen sculpture.
   C. Nothing is around the broken sculpture, showing that Ozymandias' works have not outlasted time.
   D. The desert is bigger than the colossal wreck.

43. In lines 10–11, when the speaker says "Look on my works, ye Mighty, and despair!" what point is he making?

   A. This sculpture and plaque are truly amazing.
   B. It is coincidental that it has crumbled.
   C. It is ironic because there is nothing left to despair, because even his tributes to himself have crumbled.
   D. Ozymandias should have been feared because he was evil.

44. The poet's purpose is likely to

   A. describe Ozymandias and his arrogance.
   B. show that even the most accomplished king, or threatening king, ends up with the same fate—death.
   C. tell a story about the traveler.
   D. pay tribute to the great king Ozymandias.

If there is still time remaining, you may review your answers.

Reading Practice
ANSWER KEY—TEST 2

1. B
2. A
3. C
4. A
5. See Answers and Explanations
6. C
7. A
8. C
9. C
10. See Answers and Explanations
11. C
12. C
13. D
14. A
15. D

16. C
17. D
18. C
19. See Answers and Explanations
20. A
21. D
22. C
23. See Answers and Explanations
24. D
25. A
26. C
27. C
28. B
29. See Answers and Explanations
30. C

31. A
32. A
33. D
34. A
35. See Answers and Explanations
36. C
37. D
38. B
39. See Answers and Explanations
40. B
41. A
42. C
43. C
44. B

ANSWERS AND EXPLANATIONS

READING PRACTICE

1. **(B)** a narrative essay

   Keeping in mind that *narrative* means to "tell a story," B seems the obvious choice. This was not really comparing and contrasting or persuading. It was descriptive but not of any one particular element, which is what a descriptive essay will do.

2. **(A)** dictionary

   Both a thesaurus and a dictionary are books that deal with words, but the only one that has that type of information about the words is a dictionary.

3. **(C)** one that has changed, people no longer trade or return favors.

   This is a detail question that can be found in paragraph 4.

4. **(A)** that despite any hardships he or his family had had, his family members lived a long time.

   This answer is the one that seems most logical, even though it is not directly stated. Choice B does not seem correct, as he does not seem to have had as hard a life. C loses its appeal in the second part of the sentence. D seems like a distracter with the mention of being "healthy."

5. Make sure you provide the two separate and specific parts to get 2/2 points.

   Sample answer:

   1. The author means that in his time, there was more respect and care among people.
   2. He talks about how they had to rely on each other to survive and he talks about living on very small means, for example, by making their own clothes.

6. **(C)** To narrate his own personal account as a slave.

   These choices are challenging. Based on question 1, we can exclude A. Choice B is partially true, and he does describe. D may also be true, but we can't make that large of an assumption without any evidence. C is a better choice than B, because of the storylike quality of the piece.

7. **(A)** The author makes clear that he is gathering information from outside sources, further citing information from soccer associations.

   This one looks complicated because of the lengthy choices, but if you read carefully, you'll see that B, C, and D are all simply incorrect and are not supported in the text.

8. **(C)** to reduce laws, rules, etc. to a code

   Based on the context in paragraph 3 about soccer rules, choice D is clearly the best choice.

9. **(C)** Not only is football (soccer) a popular sport unifying its fans, but it has been around for a number of years, undergoing an evolution into what it is today.

This is a classic example of "the longer answer is the right one." Options A and B are untrue, and D is too specific to represent the entire article.

10. This question requires three elements: a graphic and two examples of support.

Sample answer:

   1. A time line showing the changes that occurred over time would help a reader more clearly understand the ideas.
   2. There were many dates mentioned and a time line would help the reader to track the changes throughout the history of soccer.
   3. Soccer has been around for many, many years, and a time line would emphasize that.

11. **(C)** The researcher has done research using a variety of sources.

In this case, the only logical way for a researcher to know the specific dates in regard to the origin of soccer would be research. The other choices are either unreasonable or not a way to find out reliable information.

12. **(C)** The reader does not expect to see that football is widely considered to be the final proximate cause in the Football War in June 1969 between El Salvador and Honduras.

Although the other choices are interesting, the only detail that qualifies as "surprising" is that football caused a war.

13. **(D)** The game began in the 2nd and 3rd centuries. However, the rules have changed from a disorderly sport, to a more regulated sport.

To answer this question correctly, you must focus on the word "evolved." This should give you an image of changing and growing wiser. This being the case, the change from "disorderly" to "more regulated" qualifies as the best choice.

14. **(A)** According to a survey conducted by FIFA and published in the spring of 2001, over 240 million people regularly play football in more than 200 countries in every part of the world.

Choice B does not refer to affecting people. C refers to people who might play soccer. D is perhaps true, but not really mentioned specifically in the piece and too broad to be the correct answer.

15. **(D)** to choose as a standard or required in a course

Choice A is a distracter that is the most common definition of "adopted" and is there for anyone to choose who does not take the time to read the question carefully. B and C involve changing and correctness, which are not indicated in the sentence.

16. **(C)** The puppy hobbles, and the boy has a leg brace, and they will understand each other.

    Neither A nor B is supported in the text. D sounds partially true, but there is no mention of the boy's "maturity."

17. **(D)** ungraceful

    If you look back at the context of paragraph 7, this word is used in relation to the puppy's movement or "hobbling." A and B are simply incorrect, and C does not properly match the context.

18. **(C)** to provide a climax to the story

    This takes you back to our discussion of the parts of a good story. Because it is right at the highest point in the story, climax fits best. There is a resolution that follows, this is too far in to be background, and it is not strong enough to qualify as irony.

19. Sample answer:

    1. The boy rolls up his pants.
    2. He shows the farmer that he has a leg brace.
    3. He tells the farmer about not being able to run well.
    4. He explains to the farmer that the hobbling dog will understand him.

20. **(A)** the puppy will not be able to "run and play like the other dogs would."

    Choices B and C are not supported in the text. D is true, but it is not why the farmer says this. A is supported in the text, which is easy to see if you look back to check your answer.

21. **(D)** who need someone who understands.

    This is a detail question. If you take the time to look it up, you are sure to get it right. This quote appears in the last line of the piece.

22. **(C)** no man or woman escapes death.

    Choice D is simply incorrect. A and B are too simplistic to be correct. They are merely mentioned in the poem.

23. Sample answer:

    1. In the poem, *haste* is used to mean "rush" or "hurry."
    2. The context clue is that this follows the speaker saying that Death "slowly drove" and that he "knew no haste."

24. **(D)** Because I could not stop for Death, / He kindly stopped for me;

    Choice A describes the action of the poem. B describes the feelings. C describes scenery. D refers specifically to Death stopping even though the speaker was not waiting for Death.

Reading Practice—Test 2

25. **(A)** any thin, light fabric

All of the choices involve fabric, so that's not much help. But the speaker talks about feeling a "chill." Since B is about a "heavy" cloth, that's out. C and D are not supported in the text.

26. **(C)** death is unavoidable.

Choice A is the opposite. B is not supported by the poem. C is mentioned in the last stanza but in regard to the speaker going to "eternity." Overall, death in the poem is unavoidable and inevitable.

27. **(C)** the observations of a someone dying. He/She is taken by death; he/she observes life going on without him/her. Then he/she finally rests in the ground in his/her grave.

Choices A and B are not supported in the text. D mentions "Death coming," but for most of the poem Death is already there, making C the better of the two.

28. **(B)** the narrator's final "home" is the grave.

Given that the poem is about death, B is clearly the best choice.

29. Sample answer:
   1. The author shows that death is unavoidable by having Death be in control during the entire poem.
   2. Death stops to pick up the speaker even though she didn't stop for Death.
   3. Death drives the carriage and takes the speaker wherever he chooses.
   4. Death drops the speaker off at her grave, indicated that is where she will stay.

30. **(C)** Death is courteous.

Choices A, B, and D are not supported in the text. Putting away one's work is a sign of being courteous.

31. **(A)** Theodoric had already noted with growing terror the recurring stacks of small, ugly dwellings that heralded the journey's end. The words acted as a signal. Like a hunted beast breaking cover and dashing madly toward some other haven of momentary safety he threw aside his rug, and struggled frantically into his disheveled garments.

Choice B does not show "helplessness." C shows the woman's helplessness, and D does not show "helplessness" at all.

32. **(A)** She is blind.

Choice B means unemotional. C is untrue in the story, and D is unlikely in the story.

33. **(D)** fearful

This is where the train is pulling into the station, and Theodoric is still not dressed. D seems the most logical choice given the description in paragraph 17.

34. **(A)** Jumping to conclusions can create the wrong conclusions.

    Considering that Theodoric went through all of his embarrassment and nervousness about being seen and it turns out the woman can't see him (all of which was jumping to conclusions), A seems the most logical choice.

35. Sample answer:

    1. The author develops suspense in the story using Theodoric's fear and embarrassment.
    2. Theodoric is afraid that the woman will see him not fully dressed trying to get rid of the mouse.
    3. He puts the curtain up but is embarrassed when it falls and wakes up the woman.
    4. He is not sure he will be able to get dressed before the train pulls into the crowded station since the woman will not fall back asleep.

36. **(C)** to explain how the mouse arrived onto the train

    The mouse was a key part of the story, as it causes all of the humor and suspense. That being the case, it is important that the author provide an explanation of how the mouse ended up in Theodoric's clothing. A and B are not key elements to the story, and D does not have to take place at the stable to be shown to the reader.

37. **(D)** extremely bold or daring; recklessly brave.

    Since this word is in regard to Theodoric undressing in front of a woman to rid himself of the mouse, D is the best response. Looking back at the context in paragraph 1 would have made this obvious.

38. **(B)** It shows he is afraid of the smallest problems in life.

    Considering that Theodoric is going through all of this because of a mouse and his fear of being embarrassed, B seems a logical choice. A is an opposite. C mentions killing a mouse, which is not what he wants. D mentions people with disabilities, but he doesn't know yet that the woman is blind.

39. Sample answer:

    1. Theodoric's behavior emphasizes his misunderstanding of the "realities of life" by showing how he is extremely upset by minor things.
    2. He despises mice and is panicked when he finds one on him.
    3. He spends a lot of time worrying about what to do and about taking off his clothes, which is the first thing most people might do.
    4. He is afraid to be seen without all of his formal clothing even though the woman is sleeping and even though it's the only way to remove the mouse.

40. **(B)** The sneer and wrinkled lip will be remembered more than the great deeds Ozymandias feels he accomplished.

    If you look back at lines 3–7, which you must do in order to be sure, you will see that the sculpture read the passions well that still survive. This indicates that it remains. A and C are about the sculptor himself. D is the opposite of the correct answer.

Reading Practice—Test 2

41. **(A)** Everything becomes dust in the end.

Choice D is too specific to be a theme. C focuses too much on the desert for a theme. Themes are meant to be stated universally. B has the same problem because it mentions an "empire."

42. **(C)** Nothing is around the broken sculpture, showing that Ozymandias' works have not outlasted time.

Choice C goes along with the agreed upon theme in the previous question. D is too specific, as is B. A does not seem to be a logical choice because of its reference to the sculpture.

43. **(C)** It is ironic because there is nothing left to despair, because even his tributes to himself have crumbled.

Choice A is too simplistic. B does not match the theme if it uses the word "coincidental." D is too extreme with its use of the word "evil."

44. **(B)** show that even the most accomplished king, or threatening king, ends up with the same fate—death.

Choice A is too specific. C is true, but not significant enough for the purpose. D is unlikely because of the description of what happens to the king and his legacy.

PART 4

TWO PRACTICE OGT TESTS IN WRITING

Writing Practice
ANSWER SHEET—TEST 1

1 Write your response to question 1 in the space below (page 1 of 4).

Writing Practice
ANSWER SHEET—TEST 1

1 (page 2 of 4).

_____

_____

_____

_____

_____

_____

_____

_____

_____

_____

_____

_____

_____

_____

_____

_____

_____

_____

_____

_____

_____

_____

_____

_____

1 (page 3 of 4).

Writing Practice
ANSWER SHEET—TEST 1

1 (page 4 of 4).

_____

_____

_____

_____

_____

_____

_____

_____

_____

_____

_____

_____

_____

_____

_____

_____

_____

_____

_____

_____

_____

_____

_____

Writing Practice
ANSWER SHEET—TEST 1

2 (A) (B) (C) (D)

3 (A) (B) (C) (D)

4 (A) (B) (C) (D)

5 (A) (B) (C) (D)

6 (A) (B) (C) (D)

7 Write your response to question 7 in the space below.

_____

_____

_____

_____

_____

_____

_____

_____

_____

_____

_____

_____

_____

_____

_____

_____

_____

_____

Writing Practice

ANSWER SHEET—TEST 1

8 Ⓐ Ⓑ Ⓒ Ⓓ

9 Ⓐ Ⓑ Ⓒ Ⓓ

10 Ⓐ Ⓑ Ⓒ Ⓓ

11 Ⓐ Ⓑ Ⓒ Ⓓ

12 Ⓐ Ⓑ Ⓒ Ⓓ

Writing Practice
ANSWER SHEET–TEST 1

13 Write your response to question 13 in the space below (page 1 of 4).

_____

_____

_____

_____

_____

_____

_____

_____

_____

_____

_____

_____

_____

_____

_____

_____

_____

_____

_____

_____

_____

_____

_____

_____

Writing Practice

ANSWER SHEET—TEST 1

13 (page 2 of 4).

_____

_____

_____

_____

_____

_____

_____

_____

_____

_____

_____

_____

_____

_____

_____

_____

_____

_____

_____

_____

_____

_____

_____

Writing Practice

ANSWER SHEET—TEST 1

13 (page 3 of 4).

_____

_____

_____

_____

_____

_____

_____

_____

_____

_____

_____

_____

_____

_____

_____

_____

_____

_____

_____

_____

_____

_____

Writing Practice
ANSWER SHEET—TEST 1

13 (page 4 of 4).

Writing Practice

Writing Practice Test 1

Directions: The writing test consists of two writing-prompt questions, 10 multiple-choice questions, and one short-answer question. The maximum time allowed for the entire test is 2 1/2 hours. You may answer the questions in any order, but plan your time so that you have enough time to complete the second writing-prompt question, which is at the end of the test. You may refer to the questions as often as necessary.

For writing-prompt questions, space is provided for prewriting activities. Nothing written in this space will be scored.

Make sure the draft you want scored is written in the lined section of the Answer Sheets. Your draft needs to be legible to be scored. It may be in printed or cursive handwriting.

Revision and editing are encouraged, although for the purposes of this test, you will not be able to use reference materials. Erasing, crossing out, and other editing changes may be made right on your draft in the Answer Sheets. You do not have to use all of the space provided in your Answer Sheets, but be sure your answer is complete. You may refer to the question as often as necessary.

For multiple-choice questions, most questions are associated with a brief paragraph or a sentence. Some of the questions are clustered together; others stand alone. After reading the paragraph and question, choose the best answer and blacken the corresponding space in your Answer Document. If you want to change an answer, make sure that you erase the old answer completely.

For the short-answer question, write your answer on the Answer Sheets in the space provided. You do not have to use all of the space provided in your Answer Sheets, but be sure your answer is complete. You may refer to the question as often as necessary.

1. To ensure that "No Child is Left Behind" (George W. Bush), politicians believe that it is necessary to give each student a test each year to determine student advancement. This test would be the sole determiner of advancement. Should you pass, you would advance to the next grade level with the rest of the class; should you fail, you would remain in your current grade.

   State and defend your position on this issue to an audience of politicians. Be sure to include specific reasons to support your position. Write your response in the space provided on the Answer Sheets. (18 points)

PREWRITING

Important! Use the space below only to plan and practice your response. Nothing you write in the space below will be scored.

_____

_____

_____

_____

_____

_____

_____

_____

_____

_____

_____

_____

_____

_____

_____

_____

_____

_____

2. Read the sentence. Choose the correct way to revise and/or edit the sentence without changing the meaning.

   In the city the garbage men will visit twice a week so that neighborhoods can remain clean and so that the neighborhoods can be sanitary.

   A. The garbage men will visit city neighborhoods in order to keep them clean and so that the neighborhoods can be sanitary twice a week.
   B. The garbage men will visit city neighborhoods twice a week so that neighborhoods can remain clean and sanitary.
   C. To remain clean and sanitary, garbage men will visit city neighborhoods twice a week.
   D. Twice a week, garbage men will visit city neighborhoods so that neighborhoods can remain clean and can remain sanitary.

3. Select the correct revision to the underlined portion of the sentence below.

   Harper Lee, <u>the Author of the book</u> *To Kill a Mockingbird*, is a widely respected author who hasn't written another book since.

   A. the author of the Book
   B. the Author of the Book
   C. the author of the book
   D. the author of the books

Read the draft paragraph and answer questions 4–6.

   1. Many supermarkets contain various departments for the customer's eating needs. 2. Produce and meat departments offer varieties of fresh foods and vegetarian choices in some. 3. Others offer baking needs and their dishes. 4. Rolling a cart helps people carry many foods throughout the store and putting foods in it. 5. Supermarkets have made shopping easier.

4. In the context of the paragraph, what is the correct way to revise sentence 2?

   A. In some departments such as the meat and produce department, fresh foods and vegetarian are choices.
   B. Some choices in some departments, fresh foods are produce and meat.
   C. The produce and meat departments offer varieties of fresh foods and vegetarian choices.
   D. Choices in some, produce and meat offer varieties of fresh foods and vegetarian choices.

5. In the context of the paragraph, what is the correct way to revise sentence 4?

   A. People carry many foods throughout the store by rolling a cart and putting food in it.
   B. Rolling a cart and putting food in it, helps foods be carried by people.
   C. Putting food in it, and carrying a cart, helps people roll around their food.
   D. Helping people carrying food throughout the store are rolling carts.

6. Which would not be appropriate to include when expanding on ideas in the paragraph?

   A. details about the selections of food that could be offered in each department
   B. details about the other departments of the grocery store
   C. details about the owner of supermarkets
   D. details about vegetarian and nonvegetarian choices

7. Your school has decided to discontinue prom, citing that prom night could be a dangerous night for those who attend.

   You are planning on addressing the student council concerning the issue. Write two arguments you would use to either support or oppose the discontinuance of prom. Write your response in the space provided on the Answer Sheets. (2 points)

8. You are planning to write a paper about how the dress code has affected student performance. What should be your first step?

   A. Begin to outline information about dress code impacts.
   B. Send out a survey to gather student opinions.
   C. Research studies that show how the dress code may have affected student performance.
   D. Interview teachers to determine their opinions.

9. Which sentence would be an appropriate closing sentence for an essay?

   A. Benjamin Franklin was the inventor of the first circulation library.
   B. Ben Franklin has contributed to society in three ways, all three of which will be explored.
   C. Benjamin Franklin was mentioned in *Fahrenheit 451*.
   D. Although Benjamin Franklin was known for his amalgamation of experiments, it is his impact on American History that has earned him merit in Ray Bradbury's *Fahrenheit 451*.

Use the information below to find the appropriate answer for question 10.

- A simple sentence contains a subject and a predicate that make a complete thought. (I like cowbells.)

- A compound sentence contains two or more independent or main clauses joined by a comma preceding a conjunction or by a semicolon. (Reginald loves baseball, and Sally loves soccer.)

- A complex sentence contains one independent or main clause and one or more dependent or subordinate clauses. (Though green is a pretty color, I prefer blue.)

10. Which is a correct complex sentence?

   A. Alexander likes to eat cheese.
   B. Alexander likes to eat cheese, and Sarah likes to eat pepperoni.
   C. Alexander likes to each cheese and pepperoni.
   D. Although Alexander likes to eat cheese, Jacob likes to drink milk.

11. Which topic fits with this graphic organizer?

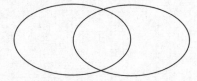

   A. weighing the pros and cons of a persuasive topic
   B. illustrating the life cycle of plants
   C. outlining an essay from the introduction to the conclusion
   D. comparing a democratic government to a communistic government

Use the following information from a handbook on language to answer question 12.

- Use a semicolon to join two or more independent or main clauses that are not connected by a coordinating conjunction.

- Coordinating conjunctions are: *and, but, or, nor, for, so,* and *yet.*

- Use a semicolon before a conjunctive adverb when the word connects two independent or main clauses in a compound sentence. Conjunctive adverbs include: *however, in addition, instead, for example,* and *therefore.*

12. Which of these sentences should be edited to correct an error?

A. Charles Dickens wrote *A Tale of Two Cities;* Ernest Hemingway wrote *The Sun Also Rises.*
B. Charles Dickens wrote *A Tale of Two Cities;* however, he is also well known for his book *Great Expectations.*
C. Charles Dickens wrote *A Tale of Two Cities;* but also wrote *Great Expectations.*
D. Charles Dickens was paid by the word, so his novels were lengthy.

13. Think about a time when someone had to overcome an obstacle that, at the time, seemed very difficult to overcome. Write a story about such a time. Make sure your story includes details about the obstacle, how the character overcame it or continued to battle it, and the results of having met this obstacle in his/her life. Write your response in the space provided on the Answer Sheets (18 points)

PREWRITING

Important! Use the space below only to plan and practice your response. Nothing you write in the space below will be scored.

_____
_____
_____
_____
_____
_____
_____
_____
_____
_____
_____
_____
_____
_____

If there is still time remaining, you may review your answers.

Writing Practice
ANSWER KEY—TEST 1

1. See Answers, Explanations, and Sample Responses
2. B
3. C
4. C
5. A
6. C
7. See Answers, Explanations, and Sample Responses
8. C
9. D
10. D
11. D
12. C
13. See Answers, Explanations, and Sample Responses

ANSWERS, EXPLANATIONS, AND SAMPLE RESPONSES

1. The following is a sample response that would score 6/6 on the Writing Applications rubric and 3/3 on the Writing Conventions rubric:

These days, it's tough enough being a student with all of the activities, sports, pressure to get good grades and get into college. Day after day, students work hard in school to try to learn and to better themselves. It would be a shame to see that all go to waste because of their performance on one test. Student advancement should not be determined simply by a standardized test.

First off, research has shown for years that standardized tests can be unfair and biased. No matter how hard the test makers try, it's impossible for them to take into account all of the different types of students who will be taking the test. Also, students are at the mercy of the curriculum presented to them in their classrooms; the test makers can't possibly think that that is all the same everywhere. The test would not be a fair measure of the students from such diverse walks of life.

Additionally, standardized tests are not fair for those who get nervous taking tests or who have some types of disabilities. Having student advancement based solely on such tests will likely end up with students who guess well or even cheat being advanced to the next grade while many qualified students are punished in the meantime. It has long been known that multiple-choice tests are poor measures of actual knowledge. To hold a student's advancement hostage by the results of one test is unfair and unethical.

Finally, most teachers will tell you that students mature and learn at very different rates. Because of this, it is illogical to assume that such development can be measured by a standardized test. It would make much more sense to have the students present some type of research project or go though an evaluation process that involves observation and interviews in addition to a test.

Standardized tests may well be a necessary evil in today's society, but to use them to determine the advancement of students in school is not only wrong—it's downright dangerous. Would we use such methods to determine advancement in the public sector for people's careers? More importantly, would we require politicians to pass a test to allow them to maintain their offices? If so, I suggest letting the students make that test. I'm sure it will be a fair measure.

2. **(B)** The garbage men will visit city neighborhoods twice a week so that neighborhoods can remain clean and sanitary.

   Choice C is a misplaced modifier, making it sound like the garbage men need to get clean. A is not as clear as B because of what information falls at the end. D similarly begins with the time, which is less important than the "who" and the "what."

3. **(C)** the author of the book

The word "book" is not a proper noun and does not get capitalized unless it begins a sentence. The same is true for "author." D is incorrect because "books" is plural but the sentence only mentions a single book.

4. **(C)** The produce and meat departments offer varieties of fresh foods and vegetarian choices.

D is confusing and unclear, as is B. Between A and C, C is more clear and concise, making it the better of the two.

5. **(A)** People carry many foods throughout the store by rolling a cart and putting food in it.

This is a problem of parallel construction. In the original sentence, the form of the first verb used is "helps people carry." Later, it switches to "putting." But your choices don't make it that easy. B makes it confusing passive voice. C is choppy and out of normal order. D is inverted with the subject at the end, which can be confusing.

6. **(C)** details about the owner of supermarkets

Hopefully you read the question carefully and noticed it asked which would NOT be appropriate. The only choice that seems unrelated is C. The other three choices deal with food, shopping, or areas of the actual store.

7. Sample 2/2 response:

I believe that prom should be cancelled. First off, most people who go to prom misbehave in some way that night, whether it's with drinking or some other controlled substance. Think about all of the kids on the road that night and the potential for accidents. It is not worth the lives that might be lost to have this event. Furthermore, although not all students behave this way, the overall cost for prom is excessive and an utter distraction to all involved. Prom may be a tradition for high school students, but "what is popular is not always right, and what is right is not always popular."

8. **(C)** Research studies that show how the dress code may have affected student performance.

Choice A assumes you have information, which you don't yet. B and D involve opinions, which might not be considered adequate evidence. C relies on research linked to student performance.

9. **(D)** Although Benjamin Franklin was known for his amalgamation of experiments, it is his impact on American History that has earned him merit in Ray Bradbury's *Fahrenheit 451*.

A does not have any indication that it is concluding an essay. B is worded as an introductory sentence. C is too specific. D is worded in a way that makes it clear the elements were discussed in the essay and are now being summarized in a concluding fashion.

10. **(D)** Although Alexander likes to eat cheese, Jacob likes to drink milk.

Based on the definitions provided, you are looking for one independent and one or more subordinate clauses for a complex sentence. Did you label them like we practiced? Choice A is a simple sentence. B is a compound sentence. C is a simple sentence with compound direct objects. D begins with an adverb clause and is linked to a main or independent clause.

11. **(D)** comparing a democratic government to a communistic government

This is a Venn diagram that's used to compare, with similarities falling in the middle "overlapping" zone. D is the only choice that mentions comparing.

12. **(C)** Charles Dickens wrote *A Tale of Two Cities*, but also wrote *Great Expectations*.

You are looking for an actual error in this one not something to revise. Choice A uses a semi-colon to join two independent clauses, so it's fine. B uses a semi-colon, conjunctive adverb, and a comma to join the two clauses, so it, too, is fine. D used a coordinating conjunction and a comma, so it is correct. C does not need a semi-colon; it breaks the rules that you were given.

13. Sample response with 6/6 on Writing Applications and 3/3 on Writing Conventions

John had always considered himself a good student. Consistently, he had brought home report cards with As and Bs. It was for this reason that he was so depressed when he found that he was failing his math class during basketball season, which would mean that he would be ineligible to play—that is, if the coach were to find out.

Every Tuesday, the coach had the players get sheets signed by the teachers to verify the players' grades in all of their classes. Normally, this was an easy task to accomplish; John was never shy about asking his teachers to sign it, and most of them even wrote nice comments or even "good luck tonight!" Having that type of support made John proud to be on the team, but he was not looking forward to having Miss Bonnie slap a big old F on there.

All day John dreaded handing the blue form to Miss Bonnie. He didn't know what she would say to him, and it didn't matter. All that mattered was that when he handed it to Coach Mueller, he'd get that look and then be told that he wasn't dressing for the game that night. Of all the bad timing, too—it was Fairfield, their biggest rival. As John watched the minutes tick by in last period, he knew he would have to do something. He thought about trying to slip out of the room unnoticed, or even pretending to be sick. He decided on a different plan. He would simply forge Miss Bonnie's grade and signature. Who would notice? After all, it was just for one week. John planned to bring his grade up right away.

Later that night as he was lacing up his shoes for the game, Coach Mueller poked his head in the locker room. "John, I need to talk to you," he said. John's heart jumped into his throat. How could this be? His forgery was perfect. After John had sat down in the office, Coach Mueller continued. "John, Miss Bonnie tells me she didn't sign your eligibility sheet this week, but I see here that you are getting a B in math. How is this possible?" John thought about trying to make up some excuse, but he had done enough faking for the day. John said, "Coach, she didn't sign that. I did that because I was afraid I wouldn't play and that my parents would be mad. I blew it."

Coach did sit John out for the night, but because John had been honest, he let him dress and warm up. As far as anyone knew, he just didn't get to play because Coach Mueller didn't put him in. The athletic director sent home a letter to John's parents, and when they asked John to explain, it all came out: He felt dumb in math and was just too embarrassed and frustrated to ask for help. Even though it was an unpleasant experience overall, John learned a valuable lesson about honesty and integrity, and that everyone needs a little help sometimes.

Writing Practice
ANSWER SHEET–TEST 2

1 Write your response to question 1 in the space below (page 1 of 4).

1 (page 2 of 4).

Writing Practice

ANSWER SHEET—TEST 2

1 (page 3 of 4).

_____

_____

_____

_____

_____

_____

_____

_____

_____

_____

_____

_____

_____

_____

_____

_____

_____

_____

_____

_____

_____

_____

_____

Writing Practice
ANSWER SHEET—TEST 2

1 (page 4 of 4).

Writing Practice
ANSWER SHEET—TEST 2

2 Ⓐ Ⓑ Ⓒ Ⓓ

3 Ⓐ Ⓑ Ⓒ Ⓓ

4 Ⓐ Ⓑ Ⓒ Ⓓ

5 Ⓐ Ⓑ Ⓒ Ⓓ

6 Ⓐ Ⓑ Ⓒ Ⓓ

7 Write your response to question 7 in the space below.

_____

_____

_____

_____

_____

_____

_____

_____

_____

_____

_____

_____

_____

_____

_____

_____

_____

_____

_____

Writing Practice
ANSWER SHEET—TEST 2

8 (A) (B) (C) (D)

9 (A) (B) (C) (D)

10 (A) (B) (C) (D)

11 (A) (B) (C) (D)

12 (A) (B) (C) (D)

Writing Practice

13 Write your response to question 13 in the space below (page 1 of 4).

_____
_____
_____
_____
_____
_____
_____
_____
_____
_____
_____
_____
_____
_____
_____
_____
_____
_____
_____
_____
_____
_____
_____
_____
_____

13 (page 2 of 4).

_____

_____

_____

_____

_____

_____

_____

_____

_____

_____

_____

_____

_____

_____

_____

_____

_____

_____

_____

_____

_____

_____

_____

_____

Writing Practice

ANSWER SHEET—TEST 2

13 (page 3 of 4).

_____

_____

_____

_____

_____

_____

_____

_____

_____

_____

_____

_____

_____

_____

_____

_____

_____

_____

_____

_____

_____

_____

13 (page 4 of 4).

_____

_____

_____

_____

_____

_____

_____

_____

_____

_____

_____

_____

_____

_____

_____

_____

_____

_____

_____

_____

_____

_____

_____

_____

Writing Practice

Writing Practice Test 2

Directions: The writing test consists of two writing-prompt questions, 10 multiple-choice questions, and one short-answer question. The maximum time allowed for the entire test is 2 1/2 hours. You may answer the questions in any order, but plan your time so that you have enough time to complete the second writing-prompt question, which is at the end of the test. You may refer to the questions as often as necessary.

For writing-prompt questions, space is provided for prewriting activities. Nothing written in this space will be scored.

Make sure the draft you want scored is written in the lined section of the Answer Sheets. Your draft needs to be legible to be scored. It may be in printed or cursive handwriting.

Revision and editing are encouraged, although for the purposes of this test, you will not be able to use reference materials. Erasing, crossing out, and other editing changes may be made right on your draft in the Answer Sheets. You do not have to use all of the space provided in your Answer Sheets, but be sure your answer is complete. You may refer to the question as often as necessary.

For multiple-choice questions, most questions are associated with a brief paragraph or a sentence. Some of the questions are clustered together; others stand alone. After reading the paragraph and question, choose the best answer and blacken the corresponding space in your Answer Document. If you want to change an answer, make sure that you erase the old answer completely.

For the short-answer question, write your answer on the Answer Sheets in the space provided. You do not have to use all of the space provided in your Answer Sheets, but be sure your answer is complete. You may refer to the question as often as necessary.

1. In many Ohio cities, a smoking ban has been instituted as decided by the voters. However, some businesses complain that the fact that the right to smoke in their establishments has been taken away has damaged their ability to make a living. Assume you are old enough to vote on this issue. You must state and defend your position on this issue to an audience of city politicians. Be sure to include specific reasons to support your position. Write your response in the space provided on the Answer Sheets. (18 points)

PREWRITING

Important! Use the space below only to plan and practice your response. Nothing you write in the space below will be scored.

_____

_____

_____

_____

_____

_____

_____

_____

_____

_____

_____

_____

_____

_____

_____

_____

_____

_____

2. Read the sentence. Choose the correct way to revise and/or edit the sentence without changing the meaning.

Rock and Roll has evolved since the fifties due to bands like The Beatles, The Rolling Stones, Nirvana, and Pearl Jam. ·

(A) Bands like The Rolling Stones, The Beatles, Nirvana, and Pearl Jam have evolved Rock and Roll in the 1950s.
(B) Evolving Rock and Roll, The Rolling Stones, The Beatles, Nirvana, and Pearl Jam since the fifties.
(C) The Beatles, The Rolling Stones, Nirvana, and Pearl Jam have helped Rock and Roll evolve since the fifties.
(D) Since the Fifties, Rock and Roll has evolved bands like the Beatles, The Rolling Stones, Nirvana, and Pearl Jam.

3. Select the correct revision to the underlined portion of the sentence below.

In "The Wizard of Oz" the Wicked Witch torments Dorothy and Toto.

(A) In "The Wizard of Oz",
(B) In "The Wizard of oz"
(C) In *The Wizard of Oz,*
(D) In *The wizard of Oz,*

Read the draft paragraph and answer questions 4–6.

1) Many changes in nature come about during the fall season. 2) Leaves change color and drop off of trees and growing pumpkins. 3) The weather begins to cool compared to the summer months. 4) Hibernating animals gathering food and store it. 5) The autumn brings about many changes in both animal and plant life.

4. In the context of the paragraph, what is the correct way to revise sentence 2?

(A) Pumpkins begin to grow as trees begin to shed their changing leaves.
(B) Pumpkins grow on trees that change their leaves and then drop.
(C) The leaves begin to change and drop from trees as pumpkins grow.
(D) Pumpkins change color as leaves fall off the trees.

5. In the context of the paragraph, what is the correct way to revise sentence 4?

(A) Before animals hibernate, they gather food and store it.
(B) Storing and gathering food before animals hibernate.
(C) Storing animals gather food before they hibernate.
(D) Hibernating animals gather food and store it before they hibernate.

6. Which would be the most appropriate to include when expanding on ideas in the paragraph?

(A) details about the weather during the summer
(B) details about bear attacks
(C) details about the other hibernating animals
(D) details about the fruits and vegetables that are ripe in the fall

7. Due to financial difficulties, your school is considering the removal of sports at the high school level. You are planning on addressing the board of education concerning the issue. Write two arguments you would use to either support or oppose the removal of high school sports. Write your answer in the space provided on the Answer Sheets. (2 points)

8. You are planning to write a paper about how students benefit from working a steady job during high school.

    What should be your last step?

    (A) Give examples of specific jobs and how much they pay.
    (B) Interview students about what they like.
    (C) Discuss your data on how many students have jobs.
    (D) Discuss a summary of how working helps the students.

9. Which sentence would be an appropriate opening sentence for an essay?

    (A) Our summer vacation was awful.
    (B) Our summer vacation was spending two weeks in the Bahamas.
    (C) Our summer vacation was recorded on video.
    (D) Although our summer vacation consisted of many adventures, we were glad to be home.

Use the information below to find the appropriate answer for question 10.

- A simple sentence contains a subject and a predicate that make a complete thought. (He went to the store.)

- A compound sentence contains two or more independent or main clauses joined by a comma preceding a conjunction or by a semicolon. (She watched the movie, and he stayed home.)

- A complex sentence contains one independent or main clause and one or more dependent or subordinate clauses. (After the movie, they ate dinner.)

10. Which is a correct compound sentence?

   (A) Patrick plays soccer.
   (B) Patrick likes to play soccer; and Joanne likes to play ice hockey.
   (C) Patrick likes to play soccer and ice hockey.
   (D) Although Patrick likes to play soccer, his brother likes to play in the band, and he also likes to sing.

11. Which topic fits with this graphic organizer?

   (A) weighing the pros and cons of a persuasive topic
   (B) illustrating the life cycle of plants
   (C) outlining an essay from the introduction to the conclusion
   (D) comparing a democratic government to a communistic government

Use the following information from a handbook on language to answer question 12.

- Use commas to separate independent clauses when they are joined by any of these seven coordinating conjunctions: *and, but, for, or, nor, so, yet.*

- Use commas after introductory a) clauses, b) phrases, or c) words that come before the main clause.

- Use a pair of commas in the middle of a sentence to set off clauses, phrases, and words that are not essential to the meaning of the sentence. Use one comma before to indicate the beginning of the pause and one at the end to indicate the end of the pause.

12. Which of these sentences should be edited to correct an error?

(A) Tara bought a purse, and Steven bought a wallet.
(B) Tara bought a purse, gloves, and a pair of shoes.
(C) Although Tara bought a purse she was not pleased with the trip.
(D) The purse Tara bought, which was on sale, was blue.

13. Think about what you believe could be done in your city to improve it.

Write a letter to the mayor and city council describing your ideas and why they should act on your advice. Include in your letter specific details about your ideas and exactly how they will improve the city. Write your answer in the space provided on the Answer Sheets. (18 points)

PREWRITING

Important! Use the space below only to plan and practice your response. Nothing you write in the space below will be scored.

_____

_____

_____

_____

_____

_____

_____

_____

_____

_____

_____

_____

_____

If there is still time remaining, you may review your answers.

Writing Practice
ANSWER KEY—TEST 2

1. See Answers, Explanations, and Sample Responses
2. C
3. C
4. A
5. A
6. D
7. See Answers, Explanations, and Sample Responses
8. D
9. A
10. B
11. B
12. C
13. See Answers, Explanations, and Sample Responses

ANSWERS, EXPLANATIONS, AND SAMPLE RESPONSES

1. The following is a sample response that would scores 6/6 on Writing Applications rubric and 3/3 on Writing Conventions rubric.

> We live in democracy. Sometimes that works out for people, and sometimes the majority goes in the opposite direction. When it comes to the smoking ban, I feel that it was a wise choice and I am glad that the voters agreed. Although some business owners feel that it is costing them money, what's gained by the ban is far more important.
>
> We have known for years that smoking is deadly, and recently it has been proven that second hand smoke is dangerous, too. Smokers may feel they should have the freedom to smoke, but should they have the freedom to do harm to the innocent people around them? Most other things that are as dangerous are outlawed in public, but for some reason (can you say Big Tobacco?), smoking remains legal. Again, if a person chooses to inhale cancer causing agents in his own home, that's his right, but now that smoking is banned in public, the rights of non-smokers are being given equal value and importance.
>
> Putting aside for a moment how deadly smoking is, in public places, it's just plain gross. I don't want to smell like smoke, and I don't want to smell and taste smoke while out in public, especially in enclosed places like restaurants and stores. Thankfully, they wised up and banned smoking on airplanes long ago. It's simply not fair to expect the general public to endure this type of torture because of people's addictions. Do we ask people to endure drunk drivers because they are alcoholics?
>
> If businesses are losing money, then I'm sure that's difficult. Perhaps they can do more to cater to non-smokers. Maybe they can find a way to entice the smokers to patronize their businesses without smoking (free patches?). Either way, no one wants them to lose money, but money is not worth my health and the health and quality of life of those with equal rights who don't want to be around smoke.
>
> The smoking ban is here and I hope it's here to stay. It's about time that we all paid attention to what was really important—clean and healthy living for all those who choose it and not having to tolerate those who choose to smoke away years of their life. Democracy works, and this is proof positive.

2. **(C)** The Beatles, The Rolling Stones, Nirvana and Pearl Jam have helped Rock and Roll evolve since the fifties.

   This sentence is not active enough. You should look for a way to begin it with the subject. The only one that does that is C. D begins with an adverb clause, B begins with a participle phrase, and A contains an odd usage of "evolved."

3. **(C)** In *The Wizard of Oz*,

   This is a movie title, so it gets italicized, eliminating A and B. Also, we capitalize first, last, and important words in a title, eliminating D.

4. **(A)** Pumpkins begin to grow as trees begin to shed their changing leaves.

"Pumpkins" is confusing at the end of the sentence. This eliminates C. D makes it sound like it happens at the exact same moment. B mentions "drop" at the end of the sentence, making it unclear what is dropping, the leaves or the pumpkins.

5. **(A)** Before animals hibernate, they gather food and store it.

This should sound incorrect to you. The word "gathering" is not the correct tense. B is a fragment. C using "gathering" to describe the animals, which is not clear enough. D is wordy and repetitive. A is clear and concise.

6. **(D)** Details about the fruits and vegetables that are ripe in the fall.

B and C are unrelated, and A mentions a season but an unrelated season. Since pumpkins were a focus, D is a logical choice.

7. sample 2/2 response:

Even though the district is short on money, it would be a crime to remove sports from the high school. First, sports are a way to build school spirit and self-esteem. Hundreds of students would lose out on this if they were to do away with them. Teachers tell us how important it is to be involved, and sports are an excellent way to do this. Also, being in sports builds discipline and time management skills. Coaches help athletes to live up to personal and team goals, and all students have to learn how to juggle practice, games, schoolwork and family commitments. It is a valuable growing experience that will be taken away from all athletes if sports are removed. Please rethink the decision to balance the district's budget on the backs of student-athletes.

8. **(D)** Discuss a summary of how working helps the students.

The question asks for the last step. Only D involves the conclusion of the paper. A, B, and C all mention steps along the way.

9. **(A)** Our summer vacation was awful.

D is a better closing sentence. B is too specific. C sounds like a random detail.

10. **(B)** Patrick likes to play soccer; and Joanne likes to play ice hockey.

B has two independent clauses joined by a coordinating conjunction and a comma, making it the only compound sentence. A is simple. C has compound direct objects, and D is a compound-complex sentence.

11. **(B)** illustrating the life cycle of plants.

This graphic shows a circular process. That is not used to compare, show pros and cons, or to outline.

12. **(C)** Although Tara bought a purse she was not pleased with the trip.

This introductory clause needs to be followed by a comma. A is fine because the comma precedes the conjunction. B uses commas to separate items in a series, and D uses commas to enclose extra information that's not essential.

13. Sample response that scores 6/6 on Writing Applications and 3/3 on Writing Conventions.

Dear Mayor and City Council members,

I am a student at Stevenson High School and a member of the Key Club. I am writing to you today to present you with some ideas for how to improve the quality of life in our city. I have spent a good deal of time thinking of this, and I present these ideas to you for your consideration. As a young adult, I look up to my city's leaders, and I hope that you will think carefully about my ideas.

First, in order to improve the quality of the environment, I propose that we add recycling bins around the city. Some people do recycle at home, but then when they are downtown, they have no choice but to throw away recyclable items. Bins would allow them to not only assist in saving energy and the environment, but it would help them feel good about being clean and responsible citizens.

Along with this, I suggest planting more trees in the easement areas by Main Street that run downtown. This is not only good for the environment and nice to look at, but the business owners will help pay for them because trees attract more business. As the trees mature, they will provide shade for people who want to sit outside. Business owners will of course be pleased if more people come downtown

Finally, I would like to introduce a community wide summer reading program. Kids are asked and even required to read during the summer, so why not make that a bonding learning experience for the whole city, led by the mayor and the entire city council? We will choose a book that's highly interesting for all, have discussion groups and other celebrations when we are done. This all promotes literacy, and that's important for everyone, young and old alike.

Thank you for reading this and for considering my ideas. I know you are busy and that your time is valuable. As a student, I know what that's like. I would welcome the chance to talk to you about these in person. If you find time, I would enjoy the chance to meet and talk.

Sincerely,

Jane Justin

APPENDIX

EVALUATING YOUR RESULTS

Appendix

Evaluating Your Results

S o, how did you do on the practice tests? That's actually a complicated question. Try to answer that question by breaking down the entire operation into separate chunks. Think about the following questions:

- Were you able to answer all of the questions? Did you have to guess on any?

- Did you have trouble with any of the reading passages? If so, what bothered you? Was it the topic, the length, the vocabulary, or something else?

- Did the prewriting help you to organize your ideas for the writing responses? When you looked at the sample responses, were you able to see how you might have scored in comparison?

As far as your actual score, you know that the tests are out of 48 points; for a general passing grade, you need to get just over 23 of the 48 points available. Of course, you are shooting for much higher than that so that you can achieve the Accelerated or Advanced status.

After taking and scoring two full practice tests that were modeled after previous OGT Reading and Writing tests, you should have a good sense of your strengths and weaknesses. For example, you might have spent too long on certain questions, gotten frustrated or distracted during the Writing Prompt essay, or realized that you didn't go back to the text to look up answers you know were mentioned in the reading passages. Take a minute now to list some strengths and areas of improvement that you have noted after scoring your practice tests:

Strengths

Areas of Improvement

Taking a look at this list, think about how you can capitalize on your strengths. Also, after looking at the Areas of Improvement, try to narrow down any more specific information. For example, you may have missed all of the vocabulary questions. Perhaps you can go back and review that chapter; maybe you skimmed the practice exercises and can spend more time on them now.

Sometimes it's difficult to score your own writing, but remember to go back to the rubric and look at the language they use. If you don't feel like you would earn full points, try to identify where you fell short. For example, if you had too many spelling errors and feel like you would not have scored a 3/3 on Writing Conventions, do you see a trend in the words you misspelled? Was it that you were rushing or didn't proofread carefully? All in all, it's crucial that you spend time determining where you went wrong and think about how to correct the errors. Every point counts! Coaches will watch game films even after their team has played well and won—this is no different.

ON THE ROAD TO OGT WEEK IN OHIO

Certainly you are preparing for the OGT in all of your classes. When it gets close to March, it is likely that you will kick into high gear, maybe taking practice tests and doing exercises designed specifically to focus on "trouble spots" on the past year's tests. Your teachers will have that data from the State of Ohio, and they can see areas of the previous year's test where students in your school, specifically, might have struggled.

Please let your teacher know about how you did on these practice tests or show your teacher your actual results. He or she will be able to provide you with some more practice but practice that's tailored to the specific areas where this review book has shown you that you need attention.

The week before the test, review this book and all of the standards, sample questions, and your practice test scores. That way, you will be reminded of all the areas of the test, even the ones that didn't seem too challenging to you—they need to be reviewed, too.

Trust that you have had good teachers, you've worked hard, you've had support from your parents, and that you will score well on the OGT in Reading and Writing. Don't over-practice the weekend and nights before OGT Week in Ohio. Keep it simple by reviewing and keeping your mind fresh on the skills, review the rubrics and sample scored writing responses. You don't want to go into the test tense and fatigued because you stayed up late cramming. The value of a good night's sleep, a good breakfast, taking time to get ready in the morning so you feel good about yourself is not something that can be measured, but anyone involved with tests like these will tell you that stuff matters!

On test days, "leave it all on the court." Like a game, this is your chance to perform. You won't want to walk away from the test wishing you would have spent more time checking your work or wishing you would have spent time prewriting. When you finish each test, know that you did your best, that you worked hard preparing, and that you gave it your all. You did everything you could to increase your odds of passing and scoring in the Accelerated or Advanced ranges. That being the case, you can rest assured that no matter what happens, you should be proud of yourself and your efforts.

Think about these words from LeBron James:

> "Ask me to play. I'll play.
> Ask me to shoot. I'll shoot.
> Ask me to pass. I'll pass.
> Ask me to steal, block out, sacrifice, lead, dominate.
> ANYTHING.
>
> But it's not what you ask of me.
> It's what I ask of myself."

Good luck on the Reading and Writing Ohio Graduation tests!

TIPS FOR TEACHERS

My best advice for you is to remember that your students have heard about and talked about this test for years, maybe even before entering high school. They have been told much about it and have been on their own to make up their minds about how tough it is, how important it is, and how they think they will do. Given that, you will probably notice that students react differently. Some will be tense; others will act like it's no big deal. Some may even act like they don't care at all. In my experience, simply getting the kids in testing rooms and reading official directions from the State of Ohio is enough to put them all on edge, no matter how they choose to act about it in public or with friends. It matters to them, and they want to do well.

In preparing for these tests, leave no stone unturned. Use all the practice materials from the State of Ohio. Go through the scoring data that your district should have received and find any element that can be improved. It could be as simple as the wording of a question on last year's OGT that seemed to have thrown students. One year students consistently scored 1 out of 2 points on a poetry question about theme. Because I had been on the Rangefinding Committee that year for the State of Ohio, I knew exactly why—for full credit, students had to write the themes as full statements that were universal. Sure, they had been taught in school about themes, but it was unclear in the scoring of the OGT why that had occurred. You can learn much from such data.

Make it a big deal in your school, but a fun big deal. Have pep rallies and do special things for the sophomores who have to go through this experience. Sometimes simple things like pencils with "Good luck from your English teachers" can do much to put them at ease and remind them that the entire school is behind them. Remember that there is no reward from the State of Ohio for doing well on this test; they have five levels, but all that matters is that students pass. This is likely to do little to motivate students to try to score in the upper two ranges. But you may well know that your district is judged by passing levels as well as the percentage of students at the Accelerated and Advanced levels, so the teachers and administrators usually care. Consider doing something small to reward your students for doing their best work, especially all of those students who have the ability. Some teachers find it wrong to reward students for what they are supposed to do anyway, but the real world works that way—we get reduced insurance for not having accidents, and many companies reward employees for their attendance (maybe even your school?). So it's all about motivating and encouraging. If the State of Ohio doesn't see fit to acknowledge students' superior skills and effort, your school can. You can devise a system whereby you assign a range of points to the different OGT levels and offer incentives based on total scores. It might look like this:

	Basic	Limited	Proficient	Accelerated	Advanced
Reading	1	2	3	4	5
Writing	1	2	3	4	5
Math	1	2	3	4	5
Science	1	2	3	4	5
Social Studies	1	2	3	4	5

Using this grid, you can see that the highest possible score is 25—a student who scores Advanced on all five tests. You need to decide if you will put any restrictions on this, though. For example, if you offer an inventive at the 20-pt. level, will you allow a student to enjoy that inventive if he does not pass, say, the Math OGT? There are quite a few mathematical combinations that you'll need to consider. The students will know from how you've taught them that the real reward is showing off their knowledge and doing their best—an incentive program doesn't change that. You can offer different levels and such incentives as a field day, trip to the movies or a baseball game, special assembly—reach out to local resources to assist you. It really will help you to motivate your students truly to work to their full potential.

TIPS FOR PARENTS

You may want to become familiar with the OGT Writing and Reading tests so that you can talk them over with your child and be able to answer any questions he or she might have in using this book. You can find much information posted publicly at the Ohio Department of Education website.

Go to *www.ode.state.oh.us* and you will find the link to Testing and Assessments on the bottom left of the home page. That link will allow you to select Ohio Graduation Test, and from there you can access many useful resources.

Note: your child's teachers may be using this material to review, so check with them before working together with your child using these materials. Also, please adhere to the ODE guidelines regarding publishing and copying their materials.

From that same home page, you can find the link for Standards and Instruction and then access the Academic Content Standards. You have seen the tenth grade standards in this book, but this will lead you to English/Language Arts, and you can read up on how they progress as the child moves along though different grade levels and even past tenth grade.

Beyond this advice, keep talking with your child about how he or she feels about the test, the pressure, and about how helpful this book has been. Schedule time to work on parts of this book together and talk over the standards with him or her. Your support and encouragement, as always, are invaluable. I hope this book brings you and your student much success and satisfaction.

Index